SAILING WITH IMPUNITY

Adventure in the South Pacific

To Bette
Fair Winds ~

Mary E Trimble

Other books by Mary E. Trimble

Praise for *Tubob: Two Years in West Africa with the Peace Corps*

"Trimble's honesty in describing her two years in Africa, both the trials and the triumphs, makes the book interesting and engaging. It provides a valuable view of The Gambia, while at the same time showing the strengths and weaknesses of the Peace Corps."
—Story Circle Circle Book Reviews

"This memoir is thoughtful, enlightening and entertaining—so beautifully detailed the reader comes away convinced that they were there with the Trimbles on their two-year stay."
—Irene Bennet Brown, Award-winning novelist

Praise for *Tenderfoot*

"The explosion of Mount St. Helens is listed as the most devastating volcanic event in the history of the United States. There's plenty of romance and vivid descriptions of ranch life. And always in the background, the dangerous rumbings of a volcano threatening to blow its top. When it does, the book takes a thrilling life and death turn."
—Skagit Valley Herald

"Tenderfoot is a story about love: love of the land, love of each other and love that forgives and moves on, reaching past the comforts of familiarity into the tempest of the unknown where love and life truly bloom. A page turner and a delight."
—Jane Kirkpatrick, Award-winning novelist

Praise for *McClellan's Bluff*

"The author proves her gift for confronting the complexities teens face as they learn to define their identities and establish their independence as young adults. McClellan's Bluff comes very highly recommended."
　—Word Weaving

"A marvelous read. Accurately capturing the emotions, fears and thoughts of a teenager, Ms. Trimble takes readers on a journey of discovery and fun. A journey that is both heart-warming and heart-wrenching."
　—Library Reviews

Praise for *Rosemount*

"Having worked with adolescents in various treatment centers for the past 10 years, I can verify that the author did not exaggerate the thought processes or the behaviors of the teenager possessed by an idea. Mary Trimble does an excellent job in capturing the challenge both of being a teen and dealing with one."
　—Women on Writing

"Rosemount is a wonderful young adult novel about teenage angst, deftly portrayed by Trimble's skill and perception. She succeeds in expressing the many uncertainties and attitudes of today's teenagers in a way that will invite understanding and acceptance."
　—Amazing Authors

SAILING WITH IMPUNITY

Adventure in the South Pacific

Mary E. Trimble

Sailing With Impunity: Adventure in the South Pacific is a memoir.

Printed in the United States of America

Cover design by Bruce Trimble
Front cover ocean image © iofoto/Shutterstock.com
Rear cover boat image © ilanda/Shutterstock.com
Chart imagery: derivative works based on OpenSeaMaps ©
OpenStreetMap contributors
 www.opendatacommons.org/licenses/odbl
Other images by Bruce Trimble

Published by ShelterGraphics
Camano Island, WA USA

"Twenty years from now you will be more disappointed by the things you didn't do than by the ones you did do. So throw off the bowlines. Sail away from the safe harbor. Catch the trade winds in your sails. Explore. Dream. Discover.

— Mark Twain

Contents

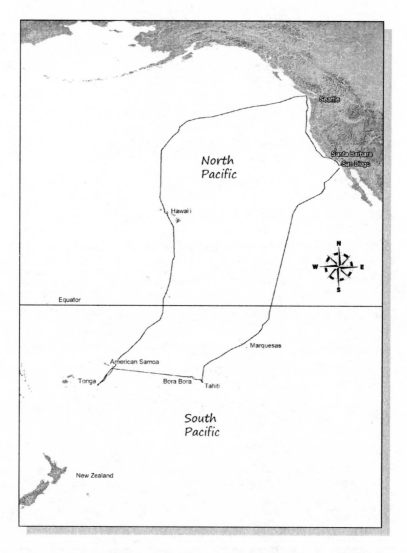

Route of 13,000 mile journey of *Impunity*, from Seattle through the South Pacific and back home.

Prologue

*T*he boat hummed with built-up pressure. We were going too fast. I hated to wake Bruce, so I waited until the change of watch to call him. Finally, at ten in the morning, I gently shook him a-wake. He'd only slept for an hour, but that was enough to hold him until two that afternoon when I'd again take the watch and he could sleep a bit more.

Bruce's eyes flew open and he was immediately awake. I doubted if he ever truly slept while we were at sea.

We were both exhausted. This 3,000-mile leg of the journey from Samoa to Hawaii would be the most difficult of our entire journey. We'd beat against the wind during the whole passage, making the boat climb each wave and then pound the ocean's surface coming down. During the past three days, we had passed just west of a tropical depression, and the stormy weather tried our patience and made our lives even more difficult.

"We need to shorten sail. We're pushing the boat too hard."

Bruce stood and reached for the overhead rail to steady himself against the boat's crazy lunging. "Okay, I'll be right up."

Once on deck, he slipped on his life vest and harness, glanced at the compass to confirm our course, watched the raucous seas for a moment, noting streaking foam atop the 10- to 12-foot waves, and looked up to survey the already reduced mainsail. He stepped to the upper deck and eased the halyard.

Leaning against the boom to free both hands, he pulled the mainsail down, preparing to take in another reef.

I stayed in the cockpit to handle the coiled halyard. I heard a loud bang, a noise I hadn't heard before, and looked up. "Bruce, what was that? Bruce!"

No answer. He wasn't there. I let out a garbled scream. My worst nightmare! Bruce had fallen overboard! The boat surged ahead as my mind whirled with what I must do. I'd rehearsed it often enough. Forcing myself to think, I went through the steps.

Reverse our direction. I always knew our reciprocal course—180 degrees from the direction we were headed. I had to start the engine. I had to drop the sails or they would work against me. I needed to throw the man-overboard pole, but I had to see him first, so he could get to it. Wait a minute! Was there an electronic box on the pole that I was supposed to set? *Oh, God, I can't remember!* My mind screamed with panic.

But where was he? I looked around—I'd lost him already! Had his lifeline failed? The waves were so high, he would be out of sight as soon as two or three swells came between the boat and him.

Truly, I had always thought that if one of us fell over-board, I hoped it would be me. I knew Bruce could find me, I seriously doubted I had the skills to find him.

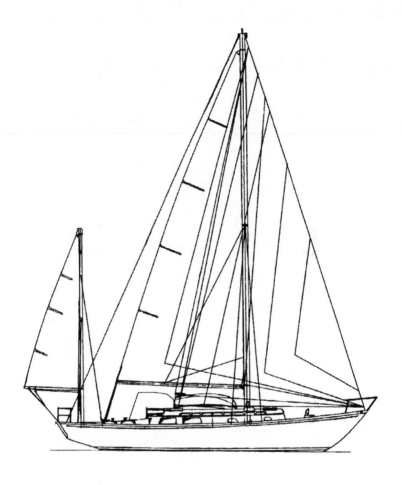

Impunity's Sail Plan

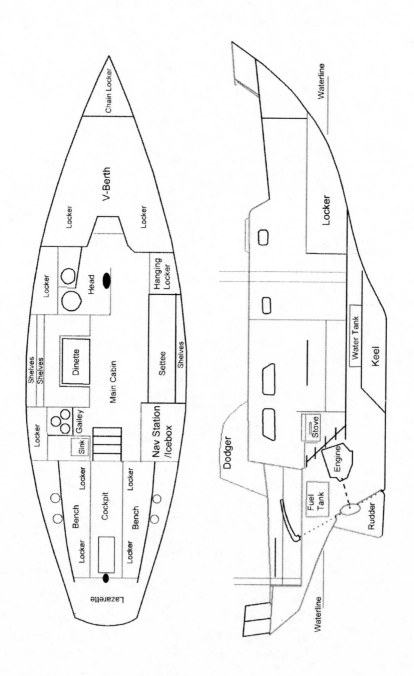

Impunity is Ours!

Log entry—October 8, 1988: We've found the right boat for us.

*O*ffshore sailing had been a life-long dream of Bruce's. Ten years earlier, when we'd been married only one year, we fulfilled my dream when we went to Africa and, as Peace Corps volunteers, worked and lived in The Gambia for two years. Now it was time to satisfy Bruce's dream. Every chance we got we walked the docks at Seattle's many marinas. Bruce would point out to me boats' features he liked or didn't like, explaining the various aspects of boating equipment.

Before we were married, Bruce crewed in local sailboat races. In his late teens, he installed a diesel engine in the tall ship M.S. Explorer, the State of Washington's bicentennial entry in the New York Tall Ships race in 1976. While in college, he had a part-time job as a rigger for a Seattle boat dealer, and in his current job he designed marine electronics. Bruce was well equipped to own and operate a sailboat.

Soon we imagined that his dream, now our dream, could be a reality. We made a five-year plan with a goal to buy a boat, quit our jobs and take a couple of years to sail, possibly circumnavigate the world.

Once we decided that we could do it, acquire a boat, sell our house, and prepare for a two-year sea voyage, our plans quickly fell into place. Not quite that simple, but much quicker than we'd anticipated. Before we knew it, our five-year plan whittled down to a two-year plan.

The first thing, of course, was to acquire a boat. For months, every spare weekend found us going to seaport communities looking at sailboats for sale. Sometimes, a glance was all we needed to know a boat wasn't for us. Other times we examined a boat closely, but for one reason or another rejected it. Naturally, Bruce and I viewed potential boats differently. Bruce looked at the engine, the sail configuration and the technical aspects. I looked at convenience, cleanliness, storage, and the smell—I can't stand the musty smell of an unkempt boat.

Finally, from a picture in a Seattle broker's window display, Bruce found what he thought might be the boat for us, a Bristol 40. It was more costly than we'd planned. Still, we caught the Anacortes ferry to San Juan Island to check it out. As we walked along the docks at the San Juan Bay Marina, among all the masts swaying in the breeze, Bruce spotted it. "There it is. Boy, she's a beauty!"

"Where? How can you tell?" All I could see were rows of masts, all looking pretty much alike to me.

"Pier 4. The seventh one down. The yawl."

The closer we got to *Impunity*, the more excited Bruce became. We were impressed. The cost was an issue, but we liked everything we saw.

We needed to feel we'd really researched the market. As we continued to travel around looking at sailboats, our thoughts kept returning to *Impunity*. We revisited San Juan Island to take another look. After having inspected so many boats, perhaps forty or so, coming back to *Impunity* felt like coming home. The owner met us at the boat, explained a few things and left us alone to crawl through every nook and cranny.

We both knew *Impunity* had to be ours. Bruce had confidence in its Yanmar diesel engine and her five-foot five-inch draft. Impunity was built in1969 before the oil embargo so her hull and decks were thick fiberglass, unlike many of the more recently built boats. She had tiller steering, which Bruce preferred over a steering wheel because tillers had fewer parts that can go wrong. The cabin had high enough overheads that Bruce could stand up, a big plus for him. At nearly six-foot three, he didn't want to stoop every time he went below deck.

Although the galley was limited, I knew that to be typical and felt I could cook in its compact space. On a boat in motion, it's an advantage to be able to have everything within easy reach. I loved the interior and appreciated its cleanliness, which was unlike many of the vessels we had seen.

Forty feet long, *Impunity* had beautiful lines. As a yawl, it was similar to a cutter but with an aluminum mizzen mast located aft (in back) of the rudder post.

The 58-foot keel-stepped aluminum main mast went all the way through the cabin deck to the keel. She had a blue hull and white decks and exterior cabin. The cockpit was large, with sail and gear storage areas to port (left) and starboard (right) the entire length of the cockpit and a lazarette on the aft deck. (NOTE: Lazarette means storage locker. For this and other nautical terms, please refer to the Glossary on page 216. Cushions covered the cockpit lockers, mak-ing ample seating. The cockpit also featured a lovely collapsible mahogany table.

Bruce was impressed with the boat's dodger, a sturdy wood-framed arch covered with heavy canvas. The dodger, about six feet long stretched from port to starboard and was attached to the cabin. Most of the boats we'd seen didn't have a dodger, and at the time I didn't appreciate its usefulness for protection from the elements.

Another feature I didn't appreciate until much later was its teak boarding ladder. While in port we would simply step down into the cockpit, but when boarding from a dinghy, a boarding ladder makes life easier. Having a solid wood ladder was superior to using a rope ladder, which many boats had.

Impunity came with sails adequate for offshore cruising:

Mainsail, 295 square feet, 7 oz dacron
Mizzen, 61 square feet, 7 oz dacron
Drifter, 427 square feet, 1.5 oz nylon
Genoa Jib, 325 square feet, 5 oz Dacron
Working Jib, 274 square feet, 8 oz dacron
Storm Jib, 105 square feet, 10 oz dacron
StormTrisail, 90 square feet, 10 oz dacron
Spare Working Jib, 243 square feet, 6 oz dacron
Spare Mainsail, 317 square feet, 7 oz dacron

The boat's railing consisted of stainless steel posts threaded with stainless steel cable. Both the bow and stern pulpits had stainless steel railings.

The main companionway entered through the galley area with sink, stove and storage lockers to port. The galley had both freshwater and saltwater pumps, and two 33-gallon freshwater tanks, plus two five-gallon freshwater jugs. An icebox was to starboard beneath the navigation station. Companionway steps housed the engine. The boat had a 32-gallon diesel tank.

Notice I mentioned icebox and not refrigerator. *Impunity* originally had a refrigerator but the previous owner got so tired of making repairs in port while his family was ashore having fun, he literally threw it overboard while in Central America. He claimed it was the best move he ever made. The family no longer relied on eating like they were back in the United States, and much time and worry were saved. I'll admit, not having a refrigerator took a little getting used to, but in the end we were glad to have this arrangement. The icebox, the only thing left of the original refrigerator, was used only the first few days of a passage and once the ice melted, it was simply another storage area. We'd buy fresh food when we arrived at landfalls.

Forward of the galley to port was a "D" shaped rich mahogany dinette which converted to a berth, with storage lockers beneath and behind. To starboard was a settee that could be used as a single berth with lockers below and drawers behind. Convenient shelves and compartments were also built from well-preserved, rich mahogany.

Impunity's gorgeous mahogany woodwork, called brightwork, had been well-maintained. The closet, or hanging locker, seemed small, but at sea, Bruce assured me, the locker would be adequate. Plenty of drawers and compartments could hold clothes and supplies.

Forward of the dinette to port, the head, spacious by yacht standards, also had thirteen drawers and compartments.

The bow housed a V-berth, wide at the head, narrowing with the bow of the boat at the foot of the bed, and had storage space along the bulkheads. It was a large area and suited us perfectly.

Navigation tools consisted of a Transit satellite navigation system, radio direction finder, knot meter and compass. Other equipment included was an EPIRB (emergency beacon), an Aries wind vane, depth sounder, and VHF radio.

Impunity didn't have a lot of the latest in fancy sailing accessories, but its sturdy bareboneness was a plus. There were fewer things to go wrong, with more reliance on essential sailing skill. What we saw was a strong ship with beautiful lines and functional equipment.

The owner returned after a couple of hours and asked if we would like to take her out. The wind wasn't particularly good for sailing, but we got a good feel for *Impunity* and knew we had found the boat of our dreams. We returned to the Seattle broker, made an offer and paid our earnest money. The owner accepted our offer and sailed *Impunity* from San Juan Island to Seattle so that we could have the boat surveyed with a close inspection to determine its integrity. Depending upon the outcome of the survey, we would agree on a final price. We had now taken a major step of the many yet to come. It was scary dealing with so many unknowns, but we both felt confident that we were heading in the right direction.

There were a few things the surveyor found that needed correction. In every case, Bruce said he would take care of those items, preferring to have the price lowered, but also preferring to do the work himself, to know that it was done to his satisfaction. After we agreed on a price and managed the myriad of financial, insurance, and filing requirements, we'd hurdled the first obstacles acquiring a boat

On a sunny Saturday, October 8, 1988, we picked up our boat from the brokerage at Lake Union in Seattle. *Impunity* was ours! We motored across Lake Union, passed through the Mountlake Cut and entered Lake Washington. Elated, I stood at the helm while Bruce dashed around the boat checking on our navigation systems, the engine, the knot meter. We raised the sails and shut off the engine. We were under sail! We tacked to the north end of the lake, then dropped the sails and turned on the engine to bring her into the Harbour Village Marina in Kenmore, Washington.

When we shared our news with family and friends, we didn't mention our ultimate goal to circum-navigate, preferring to wait until our plans were firm. We let them think it was for boon-docking around Puget Sound, maybe occasionally venturing farther. Never mind that *Impunity* was a sea-going vessel, overkill for Puget Sound waters.

We needed to sell our house. A few months into our search for a boat, we'd sold our "little house," our first home. We had lived in that house while Bruce worked for an electronic repair company and I was Admissions Director at Divers Institute of Technology in Seattle's Ballard District. During our two Peace Corps years in Africa we rented out the little house. After we returned from Africa, we again lived there while Bruce worked at a marine electronics firm and I went to college. Once I finished college, we bought what we called the "big house" and again rented out the little house. I worked as a computer programmer-analyst at Safeco's corporate headquarters in Seattle.

Our renters at the little house gave notice that they planned to buy their own home and that they would be moving. We'd come to the realization that we weren't the landlord types, so it was perfect timing. We put the little house on the market and it sold immediately. Now, we needed to sell our current home, a house I loved.

For a few months we drove back and forth from Seattle to Kenmore, about a half hour's drive, to spend time on the boat. We began taking *Impunity* out, testing her and learning her ways on Lake Washington's fresh water. In the summer that was quite pleasant, but in the winter my enthusiasm dwindled. My hands ached from handling lines in the cold.

"We'll get into warm weather as we near the South Pacific," Bruce promised.

Finally, we announced to family and friends our ultimate goal. Some weren't surprised, some were shocked that we would take such drastic steps to achieve a dream. Many couldn't believe we would both quit good jobs and give up our lovely home. Sometimes I wondered about it myself. Going to Africa had been my dream fulfilled; cruising was Bruce's. If we were going to do it, now was the time. Sailing takes a lot of stamina and we weren't getting any younger. We both believe that when things come together smoothly, it's an indication you're on the right track. There was no denying that our plan was developing almost faster than we could keep up.

For tax purposes, we waited until after the first of the year to finalize the sale of our home. It was the perfect house, with four bedrooms, a fully finished mother-in-law apartment downstairs and roomy upstairs. People thought we were crazy to sell it. I had four grown children from a previous marriage. While daughter Bonnie attended college, she lived in the apartment downstairs, ideal for her. Then, after she graduated and moved, son Jeff, his wife and 10-day old baby girl had moved in for several months while he transitioned from Army to civilian life.

To keep up the responsibilities of a house while we cruised was not feasible—so much could go wrong and we couldn't burden a family member for the time we would be gone. Besides, we needed the money from the house sale to pay off the boat. We wanted to do this project outright with no lingering debts. By selling the house we paid off the boat and had money in the bank. Selling our home of five years was hard for me and I shed many tears. Still, I agreed it was the thing to do. Following a dream isn't always easy.

We gave many items to the kids that would have been theirs one day anyway, sort of an early inheritance. We had them all over for dinner and held a grand give-away party. The next weekend we had a huge garage sale, selling (and later giving away to a thrift store) everything except a very few items, which we stored in Bruce's folks' basement. We decided to sell our SCUBA gear, another heart-wrenching decision for me. I had a single air tank, plus a set of doubles and Bruce also had two tanks. We decided that it might not only be dangerous to have air tanks on the hot deck of a rolling boat, we couldn't be assured of available pressurized air where we were going. We did take our snorkeling gear—masks, snorkels and fins. We sold our double sea-going kayak. It was too big to take with us.

While we still lived in our house, I put my sewing machine to good use. My Singer, bought when I was eighteen, had served me well for 35 years. Now I made several nylon sail bags, a laundry bag and miscellaneous bags for storage. A bag can be shoved into a space and made to fit in a curved bulkhead or corner where a solid container cannot. I also made Velcro straps to hang in storage lockers to hold coiled line and other small items. I made a safety strap to keep me secure in the galley.

We moved aboard *Impunity* permanently on New Year's Day 1989, one of Seattle's coldest, snowiest days on record. The icy, slippery ladder and decks were treacherous. I soon learned to wear tennis shoes and tote my good leather shoes to work, and to change them again before I returned home to the boat. The wooden hatch leading below decks often froze, making it difficult to open. Later, Bruce replaced one of the four interlocking slats with a three-quarter-inch thick plexiglass slat which handled easier and also provided more light below.

In early February, the weather turned even colder, dropping to 8 degrees Fahrenheit. During the coldest weeks, the lake froze close to shore and Bruce regularly used a big lead ball at the end of a line to break up the ice forming around the boat. That sharp ice could damage a hull.

Impunity's charming fireplace, made in Spain, had a facing of blue and white tiles. Though the firebox was small, we appreciated this little gem while we lived aboard in winter. Presto-logs, broken into fourths, burned beautifully. The fireplace, plus a small space heater, were our only source of heat, but it was adequate. Once they were turned off, the boat quickly grew cold.

The morning after we moved aboard, we awoke early to get ready for work. The boat was so cold, a layer of ice had formed in the toilet bowl. Now, that's cold.

While Bruce started our little space heater and made a fire in the fireplace, I dressed for work. I reached into the locker to pull my business suit out. I grabbed the hanger, my teeth chattering with cold, but the suit wouldn't come out. I tugged harder, quickly losing all enthusiasm for living on a boat. I heard a wrenching sound as the sleeve of my blazer pealed off the icy bulkhead. As the sleeve thawed on my body, the dampness did nothing to salve my dwindling spirits. That night Bruce lined the locker with heavy plastic bags to keep my suits from freezing to the bulkhead.

Although we could take a shower on board, it was the type of shower that sprayed the entire head compartment. There was no separate shower stall. The marina had shower facilities and we opted to use them. In winter's cold, to dash from the boat to the shower room was often uncomfortable and even worse when returning to the boat with wet hair.

The long winter dragged on. Yet, every weekend, either Saturday or Sunday, we took the boat out to test changes we'd made and to get the feel of it. Sailing on a lake isn't much of a test, but it helped us to get accustomed to the boat's rigging, engine, navigation equipment, galley, anchoring, and so forth.

One of my jobs as we neared a dock to moor the boat, was to jump onto the dock with the bow or stern line in hand to tie off the boat to the nearest cleat, It was at times a harrowing jump, but I never fell, although I stumbled a couple of times. I never did that without hoping I wouldn't break a leg. Once, when my sister Alice was with us, she was stunned to see me leap off the boat. "I can't believe you just did that," she said.

In the meantime, we took a series of classes offered by the Coast Guard Auxiliary. The classes served as refreshers for Bruce, but they were valuable for me, and my first introduction to boat safety, seamanship and shoreline navigation, We took these classes twice weekly for several months.

As the weather warmed, so did my enthusiasm. By spring we often ate dinner in the cockpit, enjoying our unique lifestyle while we watched the marina come to life after the long winter.

We took a weekend trip to Cozy Cove on Lake Washington, giving us a.good opportunity to test the ground tackle. It was fun and gave us a small taste of what cruising would be like.

In March, Bruce quit his job so that he could work full-time on readying the boat. Although he liked his job, he was ready to move on, so it was good timing for him.

As a farewell gift, the president of his company gave us a desalination system to convert salt water to fresh. The desalinator, a series of tubes about three feet long and two feet wide, fit under the cabin's sole, above the main water tank. We were overwhelmed with the generosity of the gift, and later very grateful to have it.

I loved my job at Safeco and knew I could go far if I stayed. At my last routine performance evaluation, my boss asked how I saw my future.

"Sailing around the world," I answered.

He laughed. "Who wouldn't? But I mean here, at Safeco."

"I mean it, too. Sailing around the world. I hadn't wanted to tell you too soon, because I'd like to work until it's time to go, but Bruce and I plan to leave the first of June on an extended sailing trip."

He was excited for us and agreed to keep the secret until it was prudent to announce our plans. "When you return, if you want it, you'll always have a job at Safeco."

We set a date of June 3, 1989 to set sail. Typical of us, the date was firm. We heard so many tales of people setting and repeatedly delaying their departure date. For us, there would be no procrastination.

The kids' reactions to our leaving were mixed. On one hand, they were concerned for our safety, on the other hand excited about our adventure. Bonnie was reluctant to have us gone for so long. My oldest son, Byron, and his wife, Debbie, bought us a sextant, which thrilled Bruce. He had taught himself celestial navigation and this would be our primary navigational tool. This was before GPS and although we had an old Transit satellite navigation receiver, things can go wrong with electronics.

Bruce's folks were hesitant about our going. Like any parents, they worried about our safety, about our being gone so long. They wanted to buy us something for the boat and Bruce suggested a radar detector, a device that would pick up a signal from a ship's radar and sound a warning to us. I think that helped them feel we were safe. Well, safer.

On our Saturday or Sunday sails, we took different members of the family so they could get a feel for what we would be doing. Some were en-thusiastic, some not so much. But, undaunted, we continued with our plans. In our hearts, we knew what we wanted to do.

.

Putting the Pieces Together

Log Entry—April 3, 1989: We are afloat again after three weeks on the hard.

*B*ruce's folks generously offered their base-ment for staging our supplies. One of the biggest tasks was to determine food for two years. That was largely my responsibility while Bruce took care of the boat's various types of gear. I wanted to ensure we ate healthy foods, but knew the limita-tions and challenges of cooking at sea.

We bought bulk rice, pasta, dried beans, peas, and lentils. For dry storage, I used Seal-a-Meal and heavy plastic bags. In each bag I measured enough for two meals for both of us. For instance, once at sea

I planned to prepare enough rice for two meals at one time. We'd have it the first meal with something like a tin of roast beef and canned green beans. The next night I'd use the already cooked rice and make Spanish rice, sautéing onion, and adding canned tomatoes and spices to the cooked rice. I had several such meals in mind which later turned out to be a great help when cooking on a rolling, pitching boat.

I made lists of meals I could fix at sea, calculating how much we would need over a two-year period. We knew that in some ports of call we could buy supplies, and others perhaps not. From all that we read, food in Polynesia was expensive. We hoped to buy fresh fruit and vegetables and use our stored supplies for the basics.

We'd heard the argument: Why bother taking all that food? Wherever you go, people have food. You can eat what they eat. That's true, but island people often eat what they grow themselves, like taro leaves and roots, eggs and meat from their own chickens. After researching the possibilities, we decided not to rely on local fare.

Before long, the folks' basement looked like a bomb shelter with stacked groceries, but it was more organized than it looked. Here are some of the supplies we bought:

– Carbohydrates: rice, pasta, lentils, beans
– Tinned meats and fish: beef, ham, chicken, turkey, bacon, tuna, salmon. We hoped to catch fish while at sea.
– Canned soup: cream of mushroom and cream of chicken to use in combination dishes, plus vegetable, chicken noodle, etc.

– Prepared dinners: macaroni & cheese, canned chili, canned ravioli, Top Ramen. We bought only a few of these items for "stormy weather."
– Canned fruit: peaches, pears, applesauce, apricots, etc.
– Canned vegetables: green beans, corn, tomato sauce, whole tomatoes, stewed tomatoes, peas
– Cereals: oatmeal, cream of wheat, granola
– Crackers: mostly saltines
– Flour, sugar and coffee, separated into smaller, moisture proof containers
– Salt, pepper, and spices: small amounts sealed in sturdy plastic bags
– Cheese: Mostly canned cheese from Washington State University Creamery
– Powdered milk and canned juice
– Desserts: packaged pudding mixes, jello, hard candy
– Sprout seeds: We'd learned in Africa how valuable this fresh vegetable is and we put in a good supply of a variety of sprout seeds
– Yeast: with the hope of baking bread
– Cleaning supplies: Bleach, sponges, liquid Joy for dishes and to cut engine grease, plenty of rags. Unscented bleach has many uses including as an efficient disinfectant.
– Personal soap: Prell shampoo for hair and body because it would suds in salt water, bar soap for fresh water use
– Paper supplies: marine toilet paper (very thin and unsatisfactory), tissues and paper towels for the galley

Good friends gave us boxes of freshly harvested fruit from their orchard and for weeks we dehydrated apples, plums and pears. I also dehydrated garlic,

onions and other fresh vegetables, and vacuum
sealed them in plastic bags.

Then there were personal sanitation articles:
toothpaste, shaving supplies, deodorant, and so on.
Knowing feminine sanitary supplies wouldn't always
be available, I laid in a two-year supply of pads and
tampons. Bruce was aghast. They were bulky, but I
dutifully repackaged them and sealed them in our
heavy plastic bags. For my peace of mind, it was
worth every inch of storage they took.

The list seemed endless, but in our research we
learned from others who had "been there" what
worked and what didn't. Mostly, what we learned was
keep it simple, but also, don't rely on buying it there.

We had a long talk with our doctor about possible
emergency medical situations and how to respond.
He gave us several prescriptions that we had filled for
pain and other emergencies. Our dentist made up a
kit in the event of a broken tooth, a type of cement to
seal an injured tooth from air exposure, and other
dental tools that might be needed. Plus we laid in a
large supply of several sizes and shapes of band-
ages, antibiotic ointment, hydrogen peroxide, and the
like.

Neither one of us would be taking prescribed
medication, but we had with us a good supply of
vitamins, knowing our diets wouldn't always be
balanced.

In the meantime, we had *Impunity* hauled out of
the water for three weeks at Seaview West boatyard
at Seattle's Shilshole Marina

For some projects, Bruce didn't have the tools to
do all the tasks that needed to be done so we hired
boatyard marine mechanics for those jobs. For
instance, at low tide they used a crane to lift the 58-
foot mast out of the boat and put it onto supports on

the dock. Then, they lifted the boat out of the water and settled it in a cradle "on the hard." A local machine shop fabricated a stainless steel mast step to replace the deteriorated original step. Because of previous wear and tear on the mast, Bruce cut off two inches at the bottom, so the machine shop made the step two inches taller to accommodate that difference.

We still lived aboard and I got pretty tired of climbing a twelve-foot ladder to board, rather than our normal stepping down into the cockpit from a dock.

We spent a huge chunk of money here, but we wanted the boat as strong and safe as we could get it.

While the boat was in dry dock, Bruce kept himself busy. Among the many things he did were:

– Installed zincs (to stop corrosion of metals)
– Added ground plane for single sideband radio
– Installed new antenna and cable for VHF radio
– Installed single sideband radio antenna
– Replaced fastenings on the Aries wind vane
– Replaced cutlass bearing
– Repacked propeller shaft seal
– Replaced three through-hull fittings and rebuilt all others
– Replaced all below-waterline hoses and clamps
– Applied new bottom paint, moving the boot stripe up one inch

While the mast was horizontal on the dock, Bruce replaced all its inside wiring and replaced the three halyards on the main mast. He also replaced the two halyards on the mizzen mast. All standing rigging was disassembled, cleaned, checked and reassembled.

We made endless trips to boating supply stores. We purchased spares of anything that might break down such as an extra freshwater pump, bilge pump parts, pulley parts, fuses, wiring, paint, light bulbs, critical stainless steel bolts and nuts, line, batteries, damage control plugs (conical tapered softwood plug for emergency hole repair). We mailed an order and check to England for important spare parts for the Aries wind vane. The list went on and on.

Bruce also put in a supply of engine oil, air filters, engine injectors, sail repair tools, manuals for everything, replacement seals and impellers for every pump, tools to cut and splice rigging cables. It was expensive, but not as expensive as being in a foreign country and having to send for a part; or worse, being at sea and stranded because of a breakdown.

Bruce designed a heavy awning for *Impunity's* cockpit, using Sunbrella, an acrylic fiber ideal for boats. At the time, I didn't appreciate its potential value, but would later wonder how we could have survived without it. Besides providing protection against sun and rain, the awning was designed, once its halyard was slacked, to catch rain water and funnel it into five-gallon jugs. We could roll up or lower the sides. He contracted with a well-known local sailmaker, Schattauer Sails, to make the awning and also our safety harnesses, which Bruce also designed.

We received many compliments on *Impunity*, both in and out of the water. People who knew sailing recognized a classic, seaworthy sailing vessel. By this time, I had developed an experienced eye and could instantly tell an offshore sailing vessel from a day-sailer. I was beginning to feel like a real sailor.

We again attended the annual Seattle Boat Show. When we had gone the previous year, everything seemed new and strange to me, but this year I felt like an old hand and actually knew what people were talking about. We bought a set of good stainless steel cooking pots with removable handles for convenient storage. Those pots and a pressure cooker turned out to be priceless galley aids.

We bought a bucket of fillet knives, a "special" at the Boat Show, to give as gifts when we visited different landfalls. Bonnie's husband Neil gave us a bucket of cigarette lighters, a collection he'd added to for years. I went through my sewing supplies and sorted a large can of colorful buttons to give away, plus bought thread, pins and sewing needles as future gifts. From our experience in Africa, we learned these items are highly valued in countries where they were not readily available.

We made friends at the Kenmore Marina where we had *Impunity* moored, and often visited with Bill and Alice who also lived aboard their boat. They were enthusiastic about our trip and had future plans to do the same.

Friends of theirs, a young couple they had met at the marina were currently sailing the South Pacific and Bill wondered if we would see them. They gave us Greg and Kathy's boat name, *Genesis*, and said if we saw them to send their greetings. I thought that would be some kind of miracle, but we agreed to do so.

Daughter Bonnie agreed to take care of our finances while we were away. Life goes on and so do taxes and life insurance premiums. Plus she'd pay any bills accrued in our travels. We added her name to our bank accounts and gave her our Power of Attorney so she could write checks and make decisions on our behalf.

On many of our day excursions, Bruce would "swing the compass" which is the process of adjusting the boat's compass with that of known landmarks. A boat's compass can be skewed by various metals on the boat, such as engine, wires and electronic gear.

Bruce lined up the boat to a landmark and calculated on the chart the exact direction, then adjusted the boat's compass accordingly. A compass has little screw adjustments to allow these deviation fixes.

At the end of April, I took a week of vacation for our shakedown cruise to test the rigging, engine, pumps, rudder, self-steering, galley, and ourselves. We left on a windless Saturday, motored across Lake Washington and into the Mountlake Cut, preparing to go through the Ballard Locks. The locks move boats from the higher level of Lake Washington to Puget Sound, an elevation difference from six to twenty-six feet, depending on the tides.

Getting into place at the locks is a bit dicey. It's hard to keep a sailboat still in the water and pointed the way you want it. Without twin screws (port and starboard propellers) the captain has to constantly keep jockeying the boat into place to maintain a distance from other boats and obstacles in the water.

Going through the locks for the first time was intimidating for me, but Bruce had experienced it before so was at least outwardly calm. There were several other boats and we had our hands full staying clear of them while taking orders from the lockmaster. As instructed, we wrapped our line around a "button" and tied it lightly to a cleat. The water lowered until it got to the level of the Sound. The gate opened and we waited until instructed to motor out.

Once out on Puget Sound we motored through a sailboat race in progress, then raised the working jib and the mainsail. The winds were irregular so we changed the configuration several times. At this point, I often didn't understand the strategy behind sail changes.

To port we passed Point No Point, the oldest lighthouse on Puget Sound. To starboard was

Whidbey Island. From that location, we could see Fort Flagler and Fort Warden to port and Fort Casey to starboard.

We gave the ferry crossing from Port Townsend to Coupeville the right-of-way. We actually had the right-of-way, being a sailboat, but followed the wise adage, "right-of-way is a matter of tonnage."

Strong tides at this point were against us and for awhile it seemed like we were going backwards. Bruce kept jockeying around and we finally managed to make headway.

We reached the Strait of Juan de Fuca and had a frustrating night bucking competing wind and tide. The Strait, a large body of water about 95 miles long, is Puget Sound's outlet to the Pacific Ocean. The international boundary between the United States and Canada runs down the center of the Strait. We considered spending the night at Neah Bay, but the weather turned beautiful so we decided to keep going. Soon, there we were, in the Pacific Ocean! With perfect winds, we sailed with full mainsail.

I'd fixed a beef stew and it simmered in the pressure cooker. The previous Christmas son Jeff gave us a dark blue set of Rubbermaid dinnerware—perfect for life on a boat. We celebrated our first dinner at sea on our new plates heaped with beef stew.

We set up what would be our watch system for the duration of our cruise.

2:00 a.m.– 6:00 a.m. — Bruce
6:00 a.m.–10:00 a.m. — Mary
10:00 a.m.–2:00 p.m. — Bruce
2:00 p.m.–6:00 p.m. — Mary
6:00 p.m.–10:00 p.m. — Bruce
10:00 p.m.–2:00 a.m. — Mary

Our watch system gave Bruce the opportunity to take navigation star shots at morning and evening twilight, and at noon when the sun was at its highest. We didn't find it difficult to follow the system, but it did mean no more than four hours sleep at one time. There were usually periods during the day when we could catch a short nap. I normally napped in the early evening before I stood the 10:00 watch.

I quickly learned to share Bruce's enthusiasm for our Aries wind vane which had come with the boat's initial equipment. The wind vane, a flat paddle that caught the wind's direction, automatically adjusted the self-steering gear. Without it, all steering would need to be done by hand. Bruce kept an eye on the direction of the wind and tweaked the sails accordingly while the wind vane kept us on course. When the Aries steered the boat, the tiller was engaged to a chain hooked to the wind vane.

I found it interesting that an experienced sailor can determine the wind's speed by looking at the sea. There are charts to determine this, notably the Beaufort Scale, but pretty soon a sailor can glance at the height of waves and the amount of spray the waves generate to determine the velocity of wind and thus how to adjust the sails.

To quickly determine the direction of the wind, Bruce took old cassette tape cartridges apart and tied ten to twelve inches of tape to the shrouds as "tell-tales." They didn't last a long time, but the price was right and we had plenty of spares.

Early the next morning, the winds dropped and the seas turned choppy. I fought seasickness as the boat rolled and bucked with the boisterous seas. Seasickness affects people in different ways. One of the symptoms I suffered was typical of many sailors— depression and a sense of doom. I knew, or at least hoped, that my seasickness would pass once I got my "sea legs." I consoled myself that even experienced sailors get seasick. We'd pretty much found out what we needed to know. The boat performed well. We didn't need to endure rough seas and I didn't need practice in throwing up. We turned back to Neah Bay, with new confidence in *Impunity* and our ability, eager to just have some fun with the boat.

As we went back through the Strait of Juan de Fuca, I practiced my newly acquired shoreline navigation skills with the many landmarks along the way. As instructed in class, I found a coastline navigation aid, New Dungeness Lighthouse, visible from 18 miles with a sequence of one light flash every five seconds, as noted on the chart. With a drafting compass I drew a curved line on the chart. We were someplace along that line. Then I found Ediz Hook at Port Townsend, took a bearing and drew a line from that. We were where those two lines intersected. Yes!

In class I learned how to do coastline navigation, but at sea shoreline navigational aids aren't available. It's always prudent to use all the aids available, identifiable landmarks, radio direction finder bearings, celestial lines of position, depth soundings, or positions from a Loran-C or a GPS, which at that time wasn't commonly used nor reliable.

Once we determined our position, we marked it on the chart at the navigation station, using a dot with a small circle around it, with the time noted alongside, using 24-hour time notation. Then, starting from that dot, we would draw our course, advancing forward.

When we were near land or known reefs, this process of determining our position happened much more frequently. Offshore, especially when celestial navigation is the only source of position input, noting our position becomes a less frequent task, perhaps only three or four times a day, even less in cloudy weather.

In between these position fixes, we would note our "dead reckoning," or "DR" position on the chart, along the course line, using a dot and half circle labeled as DR with the time. The DR position is determined by advancing along our course using our speed, direction, and elapsed time, allowing for any known ocean currents.

Using celestial navigation during the daytime, the sun would normally be our only source of position information, and a sun shot would give a line of position. We knew we were somewhere on that line, which we would draw on the chart. During morning and evening twilight when we could make out both the horizon and some stars, we could get multiple lines of position, one from each star, and where these lines intersected was our position. When getting a line of position from a star or the sun, Bruce would label the chart with "sun" or the name of the star, such as "Vega." Bouncing around on a small boat at sea while taking visual observations using a sextant is not entirely precise, but with care each line of position would be accurate, hopefully within a half mile or less. When many miles from land, that is close enough.

I never did get proficient with a sextant, but Bruce's celestial navigation skills were excellent. Before we left home he made hundreds of blank work sheets to fill in to calculate a line of position. Celestial navigation is not difficult, but it requires attention to details and a few important pieces of information.

Still in the Strait of Juan de Fuca, on the third night of our trip during my night watch, I noticed a vessel approaching from behind, coming very fast. It had a light configuration I couldn't identify from our *Rules of the Road* manual, an intermittent flashing amber. I wasn't sure they saw us, though we had on our running lights, identifying our vessel as a sailboat. I called Bruce, waking him an hour early before his watch. He called on the radio.

"East-bound vessel in the Strait of Juan de Fuca, this is sailing vessel *Impunity*. Over."

No response. He tried three times and still no response. We shone bright lights on our sails to be sure they saw us.

With a huge swish, they overtook us. As it passed between us and the glow of Victoria, B.C., we could see by their silhouette that it was a U.S. Navy attack submarine, going very fast, with only its conning tower showing. It was thrilling, yet scary.

As night became day, we made our way to Roche Harbor on San Juan Island to top up fuel. As we gingerly approached through dense fog, we heard the unmistakable "blow" of whales. Although we couldn't see well through the fog, we thought they were orcas, sometimes called "killer whales." They swam along-side us for quite awhile. We were thrilled to share sea space with these magnificent creatures.

We spent the rest of our week boon-docking in the San Juan Islands. One late afternoon we an-chored off Sucia Island, a Washington State Marine Park, rowed our dinghy to shore, and enjoyed walking the trails. It was early in the season and we had that special island to ourselves.

We had a few man-overboard drills. Our horse-shoe shaped life ring was attached to a floating pole with a man-overboard flag on top. When launched, a flashing strobe light automatically turned on. Even the drill made me nervous.

Heading toward home, we stopped at Blake Is-land where my old dive buddy and his wife lived and worked. John was a Washington State park ranger and his wife Jan managed the restaurant at Tillicum Village. It was a surprise visit and we had fun catching up on their news and showing off *Impunity*.

We motored back through the locks, reversing from low elevation to the higher Lake Washington level. We were lucky to have beautiful sunny weather.

Nearing the Mountlake Cut, we encountered hundreds of boats. It then occurred to Bruce that we had ended our shakedown cruise on opening day of boating season. It was a zoo with boats going every which way, lots of drinking and shouting. We had a few close calls, but managed to keep our distance. By late afternoon, it was a relief to finally slip into our quiet moorage at Kenmore.

A week before our departure, we emptied Bruce's folks basement of all our supplies and loaded them onto the boat. Thank goodness for the marina's carts that held several cases of goods, saving us countless more trips from truck to boat. Because of the danger of bringing aboard insects, we never brought corrugated cardboard boxes onto the boat. So, with one of us aboard, we took individual goods from one another, stacking the cans and packages in the cockpit. Trip after trip. It was amazing how much stuff *Impunity* could store.

We'd heard so many stories of can labels falling off as the result of moisture, leaving "surprise" contents for a frustrated cook. So, with indelible markers, we labeled the tops of every single can and every sealed plastic bag with the name of the contents.

As we stowed supplies, we noted on a master list where goods were stored:

Crackers – Forward port main locker
Dish soap – Galley, under counter
Dry beans – Behind dinette, upper center locker

Rice – Below berth, starboard
Spices – Galley, third drawer
Tinned meat – Settee, forward locker

We stored smaller items in plastic "milk crates." In many cases, we kept a small supply of goods in the galley and the remaining like items elsewhere on the boat. It all took hours, but we knew it was time well spent.

My tenure at Safeco came to an end. I loved my job, but felt eager to start this next exciting chapter of our lives. The folks in my department— about 30 or so—gave me a lovely going-away party.

One of the supervisors marveled at our plans. "I can't imagine how you would even plan for this. Why, you'll have to have a chart for the whole world!"

I laughed. "Make that about 130 charts. For each port-of-call you need three charts: one of the ocean, one of the coastline where you're going, one of the harbor itself." Bruce had collected most of the charts we'd need. It was a huge stack with most of them stowed by the navigation station.

My last day at Safeco was Wednesday, May 31st. We were to leave in three days, Saturday, June 3rd.

The two days before we set sail were frantic with last-minute details. We shopped for fresh food: crates of oranges and apples, fresh meat and vegetables. We'd have ice for the first few days, then not for a long time. Potatoes, onions and cabbage would last longer, but once they were gone, we'd have to rely on canned or dried provisions. We bought ten dozen eggs in foam cartons and greased every single egg with Vaseline, having learned that will help keep them fresh. We'd flip the cartons every week or so to keep the yokes from settling onto the shell.

We gave the apples and oranges a weak chlorine solution bath to remove the surface bacteria, then rinsed them. Time would tell how effective that was.

Above the dinette, we hung a net, like a hammock, that held fresh fruit and potatoes. It allowed for a gentle ride, ventilation and easy access.

We put in a supply of bread. At a time when everyone was so conscientious about selecting bread with no preservatives, we searched for types that had preservatives, the more the better. Bread molds quickly in a damp environment and we wanted it to last as long as possible.

Our kids hosted a farewell breakfast for us at the marina restaurant. All the kids, our two little grandkids, Bruce's folks, my sister and her partner—they were all there. It was wonderful. The day was beautiful, sunny, scary, sad, and exciting.

We received many heartfelt farewell gifts. One, a plaque, a gift from the kids and grandkids, read: "To an incredible couple living their dream. Our love and prayers are with you. June, 1989." We also received a barometer, a ship's bell, and many tasty food items. Son Jeff gave me a cute tee-shirt: "Escaped Mom: Don't tell anyone where you saw me." Our one-year old grandson gave us a fluffy white stuffed elephant. We called him Phant, short for elephant.

We'd given Jeff and his wife my old Datsun as a second vehicle, and Bruce's folks would keep our truck so we'd have transportation when we returned.

Right on schedule, we set sail from Seattle just before noon, June 3, 1989.

Although we were doing what we wanted to do, it was a sad departure. I saw anxiety in our family's eyes. Oh, as we left there was laughter and cheery hand-waving, but as I watched our family grow smaller as we sailed farther away, I couldn't keep the tears from streaming down my face.

We raised the sails and crisscrossed the boat in front of them so they could see *Impunity* in all her glory. It was a beautiful day. In that respect it couldn't have been more perfect. As we headed north to our destiny, my thoughts were crammed with family and our future, what we were leaving, and the adventures to come.

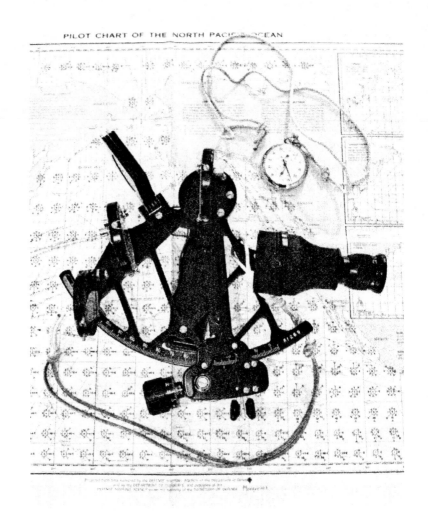

Our Astra 3B sextant

Rough Ride on the West Coast

*Log Entry—June 9, 1989: Hove to and are
riding out the storm.*

*B*y the time we passed Puget Sound's Mar-
rowstone Island, the wind died and we
motored, which also meant hand-steering.
Large wind-generated waves caused the boat to continually roll back and forth.

We both sat in the cockpit, pensive. We were taking a huge step in our lives and felt unsure of so many
things.

Bruce reached out to hold my hand. "This morning, all four kids, at separate times, came up to me and said, "Take care of my mom."

"That's so nice to hear." Fresh tears formed.

Bruce, understanding, squeezed my hand. "The kids have been really supportive."

All I could do was nod.

We took a bearing off Fort Wilson lighthouse at Port Townsend with its steady white light and a red flash every 20 seconds.

Mid-way between Admiralty Inlet and Lopez Island, we took a bearing on Smith Island, part of the San Juan National Wildlife Refuge. The island is closed to the public, but has a navigation light for mariners.

That night's watch going through the Strait of Juan de Fuca was nerve-wracking. There was no wind and the tied down boom continually slammed back and forth with the motion of the sea. I felt each jerk and knew it wasn't good for the boat. Bruce's nerves were on edge, too. We still had a few things to learn about *Impunity*, our now permanent home.

The lights from Canada's Vancouver Island were visible the whole time we were in the Strait. We noted the lights at Port Angeles and encountered several ships going in and out of that busy port. Bruce hand steered, keeping us to the right of the shipping lane.

We passed Tatoosh Island, the northwest tip of the continental United States. In the dark, the only thing visible to us was the Cape Flattery Lighthouse beacons.

The next morning we tried raising the sails again, but the winds were too light. Even on the ocean, we encountered modest seas and almost no wind. For awhile we used both engine and sails, which made Bruce happier and allowed better progress.

The boat rolled from side to side, no matter the speed. Going anyplace meant hanging on to something. Even just sitting still we had to brace ourselves against the rolling. There was plenty to hang on to with the deck railings, the grab railings around the top of the cabin and the dodger in the cockpit. Below decks a wooden railing dropped down from the overhead. To walk the length of the boat, we hung on constantly with one hand. There's truth to the mariner's adage "One hand for the ship, one hand for yourself."

It gets tiring, always hanging on to something to go anyplace. Life got complicated with the effort it took to do the simplest thing. Even going to the head was a chore and a major physical struggle. After waiting as long as possible, lurching down the companionway, hanging on hand over hand, then finally arriving at the head. Then, hanging on with one hand while with the other adjusting clothing to allow sitting on a wildly pitching toilet. Then reversing the procedure. Nothing is simple on a boat.

In the galley, I strapped myself in so I wouldn't be pitched out. Still, I needed to hang on to something while I cooked. Bruce rigged bungee-cord holders into which I placed bowls, measuring cups, jars or pans while I prepared a meal. The gimbaled stove rocked gently to keep the stove level. The stove-top's pot restraints could be adjusted to snugly fit around any pot. My favorite pot during rough weather was our pressure cooker. I didn't always use the pressure feature, but the lid could be secured and not fly off. I had to hold the lid of my Dutch oven closed with three clothespins, but I could work with that. Cooking a meal at sea seemed to take twice as long, and use twice the energy as on land. I frequently stepped up on deck, gasping for fresh air to quell my queasy stomach.

Finally, on the third day we had good strong northwest 18- to 20-knot winds. Our knot meter showed we'd traveled 165 miles. We were cruising at 6 knots, ideal for *Impunity*. The boat rolled from side to side and so did my stomach. I was so thankful that I'd prepared a hardy chicken soup the day before. Being below decks in the galley made my nausea worse, so I quickly loaded our bowls with soup, handed them up to Bruce, and we ate in the cockpit. An interesting thing about my seasickness is that even feeling nauseated, I could still eat.

A word about eating at sea: It's not like sitting down to a meal with things at hand. We loaded up our plates and the necessary silverware and hung on to them for dear life. We couldn't put our plates down because they would slide at the first motion of the boat. We learned to eat without a beverage nearby and to make a choice to either eat or drink. Non-skid pads were of little use in the wildly rolling ocean. A drink could be secured with a bungee cord, but in this weather salt spray was constant. As it was, we hunched over our plates to protect our meal from the spray.

The water tasted odd to my queasy stomach, but food tasted good. My stomach couldn't tolerate coffee. We had a good supply of tea, but the water's odd taste affected the tea, too. Wine? Forget it. We didn't bring soft drinks—neither of us care for them, but *7-Up* would have been a good addition to our supplies, though once the ice was gone it would have been warm.

Passing the Columbia River entrance which separates Washington and Oregon, we made decent time sailing under leaden, overcast skies, but constantly struggled with the rocking action of the boat. A northwest wind continued to build, climbing at times to over 40 knots.

Bruce put out a 200-foot line in a big loop behind us with a series of weights and our Danforth anchor as a drogue to prevent the stern from being pushed around into a broach. To steady the boat, we reduced sail. Each day, we ran the engine for a bit to charge the batteries, leaving the auxiliary batteries on solar charge.

Unfortunately, the anchor shackle attached to the drogue worked itself free and we lost the Danforth. *Impunity* had four anchors, now three, but each had its specific purpose, so losing an anchor was serious.

Bruce finally had time to chase down my complaint of foul-tasting water. He hadn't noticed, but it seemed to me, with my seasick stomach, that I tasted oil. That was a clue to Bruce, convincing him the problem wasn't from the water tank but in the pump. When he bought the spare fresh water pump, he had installed the new one and kept the old as a spare. He dismantled the new pump and found the manufacturer had been overly generous with a green grease around the seals. He wiped away the excess. *Voila!* The water tasted great.

Bruce listened to NOAA weather reports on VHF at least twice daily so he could look ahead 48 to 72 hours and plan our strategy.

We couldn't see land at all. Going along the coast, we stayed 30 to 50 miles offshore, giving us "sea room," a term sailors use to indicate a safe distance from land in the event storm winds push the boat toward shore.

We tried out the water-maker for the first time while we had clean offshore sea water. The desalinator could only be used when running the engine. It made about one and a half gallons of fresh water per hour. That's not particularly fast, but we had to run the engine occasionally to charge the batteries anyway and it was good to build up our water supply at the same time.

After four days at sea, I braved a bucket bath in the galley, though in this case it should be called a bowl bath. When we served in West Africa's Gambia with the Peace Corps, having no running water, we became used to taking bucket baths. At sea, I used the saltwater pump for washing dishes and other clean-up jobs. Now I filled a bowl with sea water and left the bowl in the sink to catch the sloshes as the boat rolled. Prell shampoo works well to bathe with salt water, both for body and hair. I filled the bowl with salt water two or three times scrubbing sections of myself, then rinsed with fresh water. All of this, while still hanging on to a railing along the edge of the counter with one hand to keep my balance on the rocking boat. My bath was satisfactory, but my skin didn't feel as clean as it would using all fresh water. Fresh water, however, is premium at sea. A prudent sailor doesn't waste fresh water on such frivolous tasks as bathing.

So far, our watch system was working well. Bruce was able to work in the necessary navigation during his waking hours, not that he slept much. The weather was cold and we still wore our yellow foul-weather gear. We seemed to be managing on no more than four hours of sleep at one time.

As one of us went off watch, we told the one coming on our course and anything noteworthy such as another vessel within view, or anything on the boat that seemed extraordinary.

I found that below decks my stomach was worse. Thankfully, when I lay down, I was absolutely fine.

When Bruce called me to stand my watch, it was a rush for me to get to the head, slip on my foul-weather gear over jeans and the sweatshirt I'd worn to bed, then climb up on deck. After the first couple of days in the open sea, I stopped throwing up over the side, but the nausea was still with me, though it was better when on deck where I could see the sea and breathe fresh air. Other than fixing meals, I lived in the cockpit during my waking hours.

Early in the cruise, I had tried Dramamine for seasickness, but it made me so drowsy that standing watch while fighting sleep was scary. It was less risky to put up with the seasickness. We'd also brought along Scopolamine, a patch to be placed behind an ear. But Scopolamine made my throat so dry it ached. I kept working with it until I found comfort in putting a half-patch on my butt. Finally, I had a handle on the sea-sickness.

Impunity's portlights (long windows that don't open) were clear plexiglass, but outside they were protected by a separate layer of tinted plexiglass; tinted no doubt to keep the boat cooler in the tropics. The extra layer of plexiglass offered protection from crashing waves and possible objects in the water or items from the deck that might slam into the boat. While at sea, with all the hatches closed, the tinted portlights made the cabin too dark to read. The navigation station and galley had good lighting, but to do close work like reading in the cabin or in the V-berth wasn't possible. We had other lighting, but those fixtures used battery power and we couldn't spare it while at sea. At night we lit the boat's oil-burning lamp, a gimbaled wall fixture in the cabin near the main mast, which offered a soft light, enough to get around the boat.

At night, I found myself enjoying the blackness of night and took pleasure in letting my mind wander. For night watches, we used a kitchen timer and set it for every 15 minutes, a precaution in case we should fall asleep. When the timer dinged, we'd scan the horizon.

It's important to know how to "read" ships' lights. There are configuration rules for lighting vessels and each type—tug, cargo ship, sailboat, fishing vessel, etc —has its own light pattern. By studying a boat's lights you can tell if they're going away from you, crossing port (red lights) or starboard (green lights). If you see both red and green lights a boat is coming toward you, possibly on a collision course.

Sitting under the dodger, we faced the stern of the boat and leaned against the cabin. I can't imagine life without that dodger, though many ocean-going sail-boats don't have one. During rough weather, I sat snug and dry, with frequent peeks around the dodger to check the horizon. Bruce was far more active than I with trimming or changing sails to coax more speed or to steady the boat.

I would never become the technical expert that Bruce was, but I could be a valuable ship-mate by serving nutritious meals, keeping the boat ship-shape, and standing my watches.

In rough seas we always wore our life vests. We also wore our safety harnesses which had 10-foot tethers that clipped onto various padeyes. Even in calm weather, when Bruce changed sails on the for-ward deck, he'd wear his safety harness.

Bruce had supplied the boat with a lot of reading material for me, boating information in a variety of magazines and books. I dutifully read that material for one hour during the day, then escaped into one of the many books of fiction I'd brought.

Bruce seemed surprised when I turned to fiction. "There's a lot of good sailing information here."

"I know, I'm getting through it. Remember how in Africa you turned to reading about electronics rather than reading about African culture? That's how I feel now. I need to escape for awhile."

I don't think he really understood. We had worked so hard for this dream; he couldn't understand anything less than total emersion.

On the fifth day, forty miles offshore, more than half way down the Oregon coast, the wind howled and the already boisterous seas picked up to a frantic pace. Each time we ventured on deck we wore our life vests and clipped into our safety harnesses. It was so rough while I was on watch, I couldn't be out there more than a few minutes at a time to check the horizon. It was too strenuous trying to stay upright. Waves often broke deck-level and the salt spray covered everything in the cockpit. During that time I recall only encountering one other boat and that was a distance away. Finally, it was too rough for me to be on deck at all. I stayed below decks and Bruce took over my watch.

There was no cooking in this storm. We had the last of the cottage cheese and I peeled a couple of oranges to go with it. Neither of us could manage more.

We fought to stabilize the boat in the building storm. Winds of 35- to 45-knots screamed through the rigging. The noise was unbelievable with waves crashing, the boat slamming down only to wildly climb the next wave to do it again. Anything not secured became airborne. My nature is to have everything stowed in place, but there was always something not tied down, pencils from the navigation station, a bowl working itself loose in the galley.

I didn't know what to do with myself so climbed into the V-berth and, lying on my back and looking up, was alarmed when green water rushed over the plexiglass overhead hatch. It was as though we were in a submarine. I had seen white water waves splash overhead, but not the deepness of green water. I mentally rehearsed what we would do if dumped overboard or if the boat capsized. It was of little comfort to know that sailboats rarely capsize, but they do "knock-down," meaning go completely over on their side, sometimes rolling over. But a boat with appropriate ballast should right itself. Still, damage is bound to happen in a knockdown, most often a mast breaking. If nothing else, everything would be soaked.

Bruce had just gone on deck and while I quickly replaced the hatch's interlocking boards, I heard him exclaim, "Holy shit! We've been pooped!" An extra large wave had crashed over the stern of the boat. Standing in the cockpit, Bruce was up to his knees in sea water. A boat can roll over from taking on that much water. But, besides the usual scuppers, which would have been inadequate in this case, *Impunity* had two four-inch diameter fiberglass drains on each side of the cockpit, through the transom and open to the outside of the hull. As Bruce watched the water level steadily lower, he was impressed with the efficiency of those drains. We again marveled at our boat's endurance.

With triple-reefed main and small jib, *Impunity* was still overpowered. We were sailing south and the seas were also going south, but much faster than the boat. As each swell raised us up, our speed would increase as we pointed "down hill" on the front of the swell. The knotmeter showed 9, 10, 11 and even12 knots. Surfing down the face of a swell, now building to 35 feet, at 12 knots the tiller had only a slight effect on steering *Impunity*.

Wearing his life vest and harness with a lifeline attached to a padeye, Bruce made his way to the bow. Hooking his left arm around the forestay, he steadied himself to put up the storm jib. The boat surfed down the front of a huge wave then plunged directly into the next wave, leaving Bruce knee deep in heavy green water that filled his pant legs and boots.

Bruce conceded our best plan was to heave to so he could get some rest. With the triple-reefed main boomed out to port at around 60 degrees, he backed the storm jib to windward. Releasing the Aries wind vane from the tiller, he tied the tiller in place, then watched *Impunity* settle into a far calmer action. The wind still howled and the swells were just as large, but the boat stayed nearly stationary, riding up and down easily as each wave rolled under us. We no longer rolled heavily from side to side as the wind pressure, balanced on the small mainsail and tiny storm jib, held us steady. With bow pointing westward, our knot meter showed us making one to two knots as we sailed gently southward.

Bruce gave up standing watch on deck and only went up every ten minutes or so to scan the sea. A ship can go from horizon to horizon in twenty minutes, but we doubted if there was any ship traffic where we were. Still, we couldn't take a chance.

He called the Umpqua River Coast Guard Station, gave them our dead reckoning position and told them we were hove to in rough weather and our plan was to wait it out. Not spoken was that in case our boat was lost at sea, this was our last known position.

The Coast Guardsman asked if we considered ourselves in danger. "Yes! Yes!" I mentally answered, but Bruce's calm voice said, "No, we're okay. We just wanted to check in."

I climbed back into the V-berth and Bruce joined me and held me close. I was comforted by his strong arms around me. "Are you worried?"

Bruce shook his head. "Not really. This sounds worse than it is. The boat's doing fine. I just want to be close to you. It's fine, Mary. The boat can take it and so can we."

Bruce estimated wind gusts of 50 knots with sustained winds around 35. Sailors call that snotty weather. I had a few stronger terms for it. The temperature was 59 degrees, but it seemed much colder to me because of the dampness.

I thought of the sacrifices we'd made to make this dream happen. Wasn't cruising supposed to be fun? So far, it wasn't. It seemed almost from the beginning that it had been a worry. Either we weren't going fast enough or we were bucking a storm. Bruce was grim-faced much of the time. We hadn't carried on a normal conversation for days. With the four-hours-on, four-hours-off watch schedule and trying to get things done in between-time, it was all we could do to survive and discuss the bare necessities. Right now it seemed like a fight for survival. We had given up our home for this? It's cost-prohibitive to have insurance when sailing offshore and most sailors don't have it. Nor did we. We'd heard it often enough: "You are your own insurance out there."

I couldn't imagine the boat surviving this beating. I finally slept, but Bruce only slept in snatches, regularly checking our surroundings.

The next morning was blessedly calmer. Bruce was right. The boat had weathered the storm in great shape. Not one thing had been damaged. As awful as that first storm was, I was grateful to have the experience. I gained confidence in the boat and in our ability to withstand nasty weather. I again appreciated Bruce's extraordinary seamanship. Not only was I re-assured, I felt more positive about our situation. I could tell that Bruce felt the same way. We were both more relaxed.

We still didn't have smooth sailing—the weather was rough—but nothing like the wild pitching we'd endured throughout the previous day and night.

California's Port Blanco lay 54 miles off our port beam. With a double-reefed main, we clipped along at 6 or more knots. Bruce was pleased we were making good time.

Bruce called me for my morning 6:00 watch. "Since about 3:30 I've been watching a light astern of us. It seems to be staying with us. Let's keep an eye on it."

It seemed strange to have no one in sight for all this time and suddenly there was another boat and they seemed to be following us. It was unsettling.

At sea, Bruce prepared our breakfast, usually oatmeal. It was something he could do while still on watch and I loved getting up and getting something in my stomach right away. He cooked the oatmeal from scratch. We had a few packets of instant, but neither of us cared for it and we knew the real thing was more nutritious. Bruce added dried fruit to the oatmeal. Our milk now was powdered milk mixed with our boat's tank water. With no refrigeration, we didn't mix it ahead of time. It's amazing how we got used to that.

We ate our breakfast in the cockpit and continued to watch the lights of whoever was following us. Finally, around 7:00 they called on the VHF, identified themselves as the Coast Guard Cutter *Resolute*. They asked who we were, the name of our boat, its documentation number, the number of crew onboard, and where we were going. Bruce answered all their questions. A long period of silence followed. Bruce wondered if something was wrong with our radio. Finally, the radio crackled to life and the Coast Guardsman asked, "On which side of the boat do you want us to board?"

To stop the boat, of course, was out of the question. The Coast Guard wouldn't expect that, nor would it even be possible.

Bruce offered to put a boarding ladder on the port side. Within a few minutes a sixteen-foot RIB (Rigid Inflatable Boat) pulled up alongside carrying four heavily armed Coast Guardsmen. Three climbed aboard and introduced themselves, very professional and thoroughly efficient.

"We need to inspect all compartments of your boat. Please don't be alarmed, this is mostly a safety check."

Right, I thought. I would not have wanted to be carrying illegal cargo. These guys meant business.

The officer in charge, carrying a clipboard, nodded to Bruce. "Go ahead, Sir, lead the way." He turned to me, "Ma'am, please stay in the cockpit with Seaman Turner. Two of them went below with Bruce. One remained in their large, inflatable dinghy, keeping pace with *Impunity*, but never touching it. Both boats rolled with the rough seas.

Bruce told me later that the fellows who went below decks with him searched every nook and cranny. One of them remarked that he'd never seen so many drawers and compartments in a yacht's head. They checked the engine compartment, all the lockers, all the drawers throughout the boat. After the search, the officer in charge referred to his clipboard and began writing down the particulars of the boat. Bruce handed him a copy of our "Vessel and Personal

Information" document. The Coast Guardsman was impressed. "All boats should be required to do this."

Our "Vessel and Personal Information" was on a single sheet of paper. First were *Impunity*'s statistics listed on the left and a picture of the boat on the right. Next was the "Master" of the boat, Bruce, with his name, nationality, date of birth, place of birth, home address (daughter Bonnie's), passport number, where it was issued, marital status and next of kin. "Mate" information listed next had all my information and picture. This document proved to be a valuable time-saver when we reached ports. We even had a French-speaking friend translate the information and had a document in that language.

In the meantime, the fellow and I sat in the cockpit and carried on a conversation. The Coast Guardsman still at the wheel in the RIB kept an even pace with *Impunity*, but never tied up to us.

Following sea rising behind Impunity

Finally the Coast Guardsmen and Bruce came up on deck. One of the seaman who had been below deck looked pea-green from seasickness. He was probably fine on the Coast Guard cutter, but each vessel has its own action to get used to. The officer in charge asked what we were dragging. Bruce partially brought up the drogue, explaining that it helped steady the boat. The Coast Guardsmen then inspected the cockpit lockers.

The officer in charge looked at his clipboard. "It looks like you've followed all the safety rules, but for one thing. I see no ship's bell."

"We have a bell," Bruce said, "but we didn't want it exposed to all this weather. I'll get it." They were satisfied that we'd complied and presented us with a nice safety certificate. According to them, it's rare to pass a safety check with no citations or warnings. In our case, not even a suggestion.

They climbed into their RIB, still never having tied to our boat, and were off, back to the *Resolute*. They were onboard *Impunity* for about an hour.

We wondered if our call to the Coast Guard a couple of nights before had made them wonder what we were doing out in this weather and if, perhaps, we were carrying drugs.

We didn't mind the boarding. In fact, we approved. It was our tax dollars at work.

Ten days after leaving Seattle, cold and tired, we needed a break. It had been our plan to put in at San Diego and top up our supplies, but we decided to put in at Cojo Anchorage on the eastern edge of Point Conception, California. We struggled through crashing waves, but once inside the cove found instant calm. Ahhhh, warm and sunny. Probably 80 degrees. We dropped anchor in thirty feet of water, the only boat in the cove. Below decks the boat was dry, but

61

we set out the cockpit cushions, our jeans, and foul weather gear to dry in the warm wind. We rowed ashore in our dinghy and enjoyed the sight of sand dunes and sagebrush. In total comfort, I prepared a beef hash and we enjoyed a glass of wine with dinner. We basked in the quiet, calm atmosphere. It was tempting to stay a few days, but we needed to keep moving. We never knew what lay ahead and didn't want to squander time here.

Bruce and I discussed the possibility of getting a new single-sideband ham (SSB) radio so that we would have better communication. We had with us his old ham transceiver but really felt it would be to our advantage to have a newer radio. Los Angeles would be the best place to buy it, so we took the Santa Barbara Channel from Cojo to the Santa Barbara Harbor. Bruce called the Harbor Master on VHF and was told which moorage space to use. Most marinas have guest dock moorage and permanent moorage, similar to what we had in Kenmore.

We stayed in Santa Barbara for three busy days. From a phone booth I called a friend who lived in Los Angeles and we made plans for her to visit us at the marina. We rented a car for our stay since it's almost impossible to get around otherwise. We drove to Los Angeles to buy a ham radio. It was a good decision and for the rest of our journey we appreciated the advantages of the communication it provided. Luckily, Bruce had a ham operator's license, so he could legally operate the radio.

This was before the days of cell phones, or at least common use of them. Although I had a computer, I hadn't brought it with us. The Internet wasn't nearly as advanced as it is today, and most people didn't even have email. I did have my typewriter and at every opportunity I wrote letters to family and friends. As we had done when in Africa, we asked people to save our letters so we could refer to them later.

When we returned to Santa Barbara from Los Angeles, my friend Cheryl Janecky was waiting for us with her parrot, Charlie, on her shoulder. The green and yellow parrot stood about a foot tall. Cheryl treated us to a restaurant dinner, leaving the parrot in her car. After our meal we returned to *Impunity*, with Charlie, to continue our visit. The parrot was a character and found cute places on the boat to hang out. He'd stand behind a post, then peek out at us. I've never wanted a bird because of the mess they make, but Cheryl's parrot was fun.

The next day we found a place to do our laundry. It took awhile because our winter coats had gotten wet and salty and we wanted them clean before stowing them. We bought a block of ice and stocked up again on fresh meat, milk, fruit and vegetables. A marine supply store at the marina had a Danforth anchor to replace the one we'd lost at sea. I bought a wide-brimmed straw hat, hoping we'd have sunshine to warrant it. We beefed up our supply of line.

The marina had showers and we took advantage of that all three days. What had seemed like an inconvenience at Kenmore Marina, leaving the boat to take showers, now seemed like a luxury. Lovely hot fresh water cascaded down my body. I could wash my hair using both hands. Oh, my.

We topped up our fuel and water and, rather than going back offshore where high winds were reported, we took the Santa Barbara Channel to San Diego. Bruce continued to listen to weather reports. A storm from Mexico was blowing over and it would be clear to travel within a day or so.

We spent only one night in San Diego, then were underway on June 21. Next stop, the Marquesas, but first we had to cross 3,400 miles of the Pacific, the largest ocean in the world.

The Long Haul

Log Entry—July 9, 1989: Six-hour rain squall.

*L*eaving San Diego on June 21, with the wind forward of the beam, we close-reached on a port tack. Bruce felt anxious about the unfavorable sailing conditions. At sea, it was still cold and we continued to wear foul-weather gear with warm clothes underneath.

Surprisingly, even that close to San Diego we experienced light shipping traffic with only one U.S. Navy frigate and one inbound surfaced submarine, plus three sailboats circling around. Within a short time, we had the ocean to ourselves, but not much wind, leaving Bruce frustrated. We motored most of the night which meant hand-steering.

Dolphins tagged along with us for a distance, slicing the water back and forth across our bow, swiftly ducking under the boat, then repeating their performance. Their cavorting made us laugh and gave us a welcomed diversion from hand-steering.

Although the pilot charts all but promised north to northwest winds for the area, by the second day out we bucked southwest winds. We made three to four knots in overcast weather, often running the engine. All around, everything was gray. I'd hear Bruce at the navigation station sigh with disillusionment as he plotted our course. Sloping trade-wind clouds teased us with promises until the fifth day out, when we finally found trade winds and sunny skies. Ahhh, what a relief. We began shedding clothes as the weather grew steadily warmer until we were down to tee-shirts and jeans. Then, within a couple more days, tank tops and shorts, finally tank tops and panties for me, only skivvies for Bruce.

At one point the sea sparkled with thousands of dots on the water. Everywhere we looked, we could see the brilliant spots, each about the size of a fifty-cent piece. I lowered a pail to capture a sample and up close we could see they were light blue Velella velella, marine creatures with crests along their bodies that act like sails. They live on the ocean's surface.

The trades, winds that blew from the northeast toward the equator, weren't consistent and when they failed, the slapping of sails in slack winds became irritating. Fifteen knots of wind was ideal, but eight or so didn't cut it. It was still necessary to hang on to something with one hand because of the roll and swing of the boat, but these were gently rolling swells, about five feet high, compared to the 15- to 25-foot seas we'd had off the Oregon coast. At least my stomach felt steady, even with rolling seas.

We found the midship single berth more comfortable than the V-berth, especially since only one of us slept at a time. The center of a boat has less action than either end, and the berth had sides that kept us snug. At times we strung a lee cloth that reached from under the frame to the railing overhead. If the boat should really roll, the person sleeping wouldn't be dumped out of bed. On this passage, it never did get that rough, but it was reassuring to have that protection.

One morning, when Bruce woke me for my morning watch, he crawled into the narrow bed with me. It made us realize how much we missed cuddling. With our watch system, we often felt like ships passing in the night. We began doing this every morning, calling ourselves "bunk bunnies." Only ten minutes of this satisfied our need to be close and restored our sense of "us."

My advanced meal planning and provisioning was paying off, and we enjoyed healthy, tasty meals. About once a week I put together a soup or stew, enough for two dinners. I often fixed omelettes. I found sea water could be used for steaming vegetables and boiling potatoes. While we still had fresh vegetables, we enjoyed salads. Later when it was only cabbage I fixed coleslaw with an oil and vinegar dressing. Toward the end of our fresh vegetables, I started a jar of sprout seeds, rinsing them three times a day with fresh water. I used them in salads and on sandwiches. Otherwise, we used our canned vegetables. I prepared creamed ham (canned) and potatoes (still fresh). I also creamed canned chicken or tuna to serve over rice. We'd stocked up on bread in San Diego, but once that ran out I tried baking our bread, using sea water. The first batch of two loaves was wonderful, but the next batch didn't rise properly, probably due to the rocking boat. I didn't try again. Sturdy, round pilot crackers substituted for bread. We enjoyed our fresh apples and oranges.

We tried fishing but had no luck at all. We suspected our salmon tackle was too light. We'd check our line which we dragged off the stern, and it would be stripped of bait and hook. We had a thing or two to learn about fishing in the tropics.

Within ten days, I could hardly remember cold weather. It was pretty much non-stop heat. Bruce rigged tarps to give us shade in the cockpit. At sea, we couldn't use our awning, but by adjusting a small tarp we had some relief from the seemingly endless sun. During calm seas I often sat at the table in the cockpit, wearing my big straw hat, and typed letters home.

The days seemed endless, but not in a bad way. Just day after day of sailing. I felt no particular pressure, but Bruce always seemed to be trying to coax more speed out of the sails. We fell into a pleasant routine. Life was good. I didn't care when we arrived in the Marquesas, not as long as the sailing continued to be this pleasant.

Although our watch system dictated four hours on, four hours off, sometimes we didn't even get four hours of sleep. We had a safety rule that if one of us went to the forward deck, the other had to be at least in the cockpit. Although when going to the foredeck we always wore our safety harnesses (well, maybe not in dead calm), there was still a danger of losing our balance and falling off the boat. If that should happen, even tethered to a line, the person in the water could be dragged along and unable to get himself back onto the boat.

Bruce always tried to have the sails settled for the night, but there were times he had to wake me during his night watch so that I could be in the cockpit while he changed the jib or took a reef in the main. The sea doesn't care what your sleeping schedule is. Bruce always wanted me to call him, no matter the hour, if anything unusual was happening.

Mary typing a letter home

One night after a particularly calm, peaceful day, I was sleeping when around three in the morning I not only heard, but felt a loud BANG! It sounded as though we'd hit something. I heard Bruce yell, "Mary! I need you on deck!"

I scrambled out of the midship berth and up to the deck into screaming wind and driving rain. Bruce handed me my safety line and I clipped it on as he made his way to the bow, fighting against a strong wind. He took down the jib and lashed it to the railing with a bungee cord, then made his way back to take a couple of reefs in the mainsail, reducing the effect of wind.

Sudden squalls often come without warning and can knock a boat down. Since it was dark, Bruce couldn't see it coming, but he said moments before the squall was on us that he had noticed a subtle wind shift and felt the temperature drop a few degrees. Then, the wind suddenly picked up and the squall slammed into us. Another reason why a person should always be on deck. Without quick action, we could have been in trouble.

When things calmed down, I went below, dried off and climbed back into bed. It took me awhile to get back to sleep.

We began to notice the lack of regular exercise. We're daily walkers and on a boat there's no way to substitute for this, but in the cool of the night we began doing bending and stretching exercises.

Sometimes we had rude surprises. More than once I'd no sooner hung out our daily laundry when the wind and seas kicked up and soaked the laundry with saltwater spray. I'd have to take the laundry down, rinse it again in fresh water, then wait for things to calm down to hang the clothes out. I hand-washed our clothes in salt water, using *Joy* detergent, then rinsed first in salt water, then fresh water.

We tolerated the difficult times better, now that they were offset with good days. Those early days, going down the U.S. coast had been nothing but tough, and that had gotten old quickly. But, now it seemed we had mostly good days, with a few rough spots thrown in to keep us on our toes.

With favorable winds, hand-steering was rarely required. The wind vane did its job keeping us on course. Every once in awhile, it was necessary to make some adjustments, but for days on end we didn't have to hand-steer or even change course.

Night watches were often a marvel with bioluminescence. As the boat cut through the water, brilliant algae illuminated the seas in our wake and on the crest of breaking waves. Searching the sky, I loved watching the blazing stars. In the clear air they looked within arm's reach. Sitting under the dodger was no longer necessary unless it rained. I usually sat in a cozy spot in the stern, wedged between a lashed-down propane tank and the small cockpit table, stowed upright when not in use.

There's something a little sticky and abrasive about dried salt water. The backs of my legs became tender from the crustiness of it, so when in the cockpit I sat on a towel.

One day, approaching the equator, we had a heavy rain squall. At first we rushed around to take advantage of the abundance of fresh water. After the scuppers and deck were cleaned with the hard-driving rain, Bruce opened the deck plate to fill the water tank. We took showers, washed our hair, and I washed clothes. The deck got a good scrubbing. We exposed the boat's salt-encrusted bench cushions to the fresh water. When it was over, six hours later, we marveled at our soft skin and hair, at how clean everything felt.

We'd gotten into the habit of Bruce reading James Harriot books aloud. We'd brought his first three, starting with *All Creatures Great and Small*. We also listened to music tapes played on the boat's cassette player. It was a treat to have conditions calm enough for these activities. We enjoyed normal, relaxed conversations when weather permitted.

The sailing conditions weren't as reliable as anticipated once we were in the trades. From his research, Bruce expected better winds. Still, our knot meter ticked away, indicating we were doing about four knots (about five miles per hour). At four knots, we would sail about 100 miles a day, rather than the 120 Bruce hoped for. Some days, we didn't even make 100 miles, which discouraged Bruce. I really didn't care. I loved the feeling of endless time.

On one of the earlier days of the doldrums, I enjoyed the flat sea, not being jostled about. I prepared dinner without having to hold on to something every minute. I cleaned up the boat, having the leisure of airing things out without worrying about seaspray. At the end of the day, I remarked to Bruce, "This has been a great day!"

He grumbled a response, "We only got in about 50 miles."

"Isn't it okay to have enjoyed the day?"

"It's not okay to be taking so long to get there."

"Why, what difference does it make? Do we have to meet some kind of schedule?"

I think that conversation did us both good. I could understand that Bruce tried to get the most of what the boat could give us. And I think my remark helped put our situation in perspective. He seemed to relax a little about the business of sailing. We were doing this for the adventure. All of it.

We settled into a nice, calm routine and I found myself enjoying life at sea.

A quiet afternoon watch

To keep track of our progress, using the sextant, Bruce made star sights each morning and evening twilight, and sun shots two or three times during the day. The procedure was much more involved than I'd anticipated. The sextant was kept in a padded wood box. A mechanical device, a sextant has a small telescope, some mirrors and several darkened glass shades. He'd carefully take it out and slip its lanyard around his neck, along with a stop watch. On the single-side band radio, he tuned in WWV, a station operated by the U.S. National Bureau of Standards. The station consisted of monotonous ticking every second and a voice announcing Greenwich Mean Time each minute. Bruce would start his stopwatch on the exact minute. I wouldn't have thought it would make that much difference, but if his stopwatch was off by four seconds, that would equal a one-mile error in longitude.

On a preprinted worksheet, Bruce noted the current date and our approximated latitude and longitude, known as the DR, or dead reckoning, position.

Up on deck, he'd brace himself against the mizzen mast so that he could use two hands for the sextant. He measured the angle between the visible horizon and the lower edge of the sun, or between the visible horizon and a star. The sextant has precise markings to show the measured angle. Of course, all this time the boat is in motion, rising up and dropping down with the wave action. The moment he was able to get the sun or star shot, he'd click the stopwatch.

Determining our latitude with a noon sight

Going below decks to the navigation table, he noted the minutes and seconds from the stop watch onto the worksheet. Adding that time to the exact time he'd started the stopwatch told him the precise Greenwich Mean Time of his sextant measurement. He'd also note on the worksheet the precise angle from the sextant, in degrees, minutes and seconds.

At that point he had everything he needed to come up with a line of position to plot on the chart. By consulting our nautical almanac and the navigation tables, he could calculate the distance and direction from our DR position, based on the sight information, and would then mark that on the chart as a line of position. In addition to our position, Bruce often noted the air and water temperatures..

The old Transit sat-nav that came with the boat gave one last fix about four days out of San Diego. After working on it for awhile, Bruce decided it was a lost cause and turned it off to save the batteries. We now relied entirely on Bruce's celestial navigation.

The Intertropical Convergence Zone (ITCZ), known by sailors as the doldrums, was pretty much what we expected, slatting sails and oily looking seas. With virtually no wind, most of the distance we made was when we turned on the engine so that we could make some progress. One thing about running the engine was that we also ran the watermaker. We were doing well with keeping our fresh water level up. We also charged the batteries, important for a boat alone at sea.

No matter where we looked—ahead of us, behind, to the right or to the left—we saw nothing but water, ending with horizon. Seemingly, we were alone in the world. For days on end, nothing, not another boat, came into view. Occasionally we saw a jet trail in the sky. That far away from land, we didn't even see birds.

Since we'd been in warmer waters, we began seeing flying fish and quite often they'd land on deck. They ranged from a couple of inches to about six inches. They were usually dead when we'd find them and we'd throw them back into the sea. To escape a predator, a flying fish can travel several feet through the air by using its large pectoral fins.

Once, during a calm period, we began to notice a bad smell, which seemed to be coming from the cockpit. I washed the deck and bulkhead, but the smell persistently grew worse. Finally, Bruce found the culprit. A dead flying fish had wedged itself behind a propane tank. He "fished" it out and I washed the area with soap and water.

Each day we participated in a cruisers' Maritime Mobile Net via ham radio, held at the same time every day. Once committed, we were expected to answer a daily "roll call," state our name, position and weather conditions. Boats checked in from all over the Pacific, near New Zealand, Fiji, Cook Islands, Japan, Gulf of Alaska, even boats sitting in ports.

By formally signing up, the agreement was that if we failed to report in at the regular time, after so many days (we specified the number of days) our family contact would be notified. Of course, a reason could be that our radio was dead, but it could also mean we were in trouble.

One day during roll call, a fellow called in and said his wife had fallen down a hatch and was seriously injured, possibly with a broken back. It was only the two of them on board and he had his hands full handling the boat and taking care of her. The Maritime Mobile Net arranged to have someone within range lend assistance.

Many ham radio operators on land listened to the net, too, and were helpful in making emergency contacts. Also, land-based ham operators often offered to make phone patches for boats at sea. That's when we normally called home, after the net's business. What a wonderful service! One Texas ham operator in particular put through calls for us. In order to participate, you had to be a licensed ham operator, so we were glad Bruce was. We were also glad we'd invested in our new radio. It added greatly to our sense of security.

The phone patches through the ham operators were one-way conversations, ending with "over" so the other person would know when to talk. The ham operator would dial a family member's home phone and then, through our ham radio to the other operator's, we could carry on a conversation. We didn't talk very long, but enough to touch base and assure the family we were fine.

Bruce continued to listen to high seas weather reports at least twice daily, another advantage of having the new radio. One of the reports was from a respected fellow named Arnold from Rarotonga in the Cook Islands. Arnold's report was a compilation from several South Pacific regions. The other forecast Bruce listened to was from Hawaii. Between the two of them, we had a pretty good idea of what to expect.

A funny thing about the forecast from Hawaii. Bruce always tuned in a few minutes early and shortly before the weather report, a woman's voice, speaking perhaps Russian, seemed to shout non-stop. We couldn't imagine what she was saying, but it was always a high-pitched, rapid shout. Then, when the weather came on, the Coast Guardsman who usually gave the forecast always pronounced "five" as "fife." "Winds at thirty-fife knots."

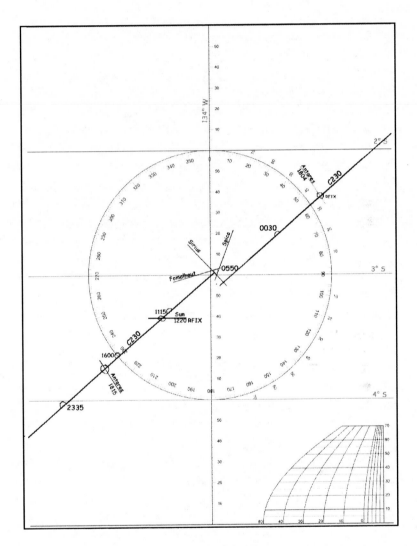

Our course and lines of position on plotting sheet

I prefer to have my surroundings ship-shape, but tidy isn't always convenient. Bruce frequently had to change headsails to accommodate the wind, or lack of it, and it was too inconvenient to put the one just taken down in its sailbag and stow it in the sail locker below. For one thing, it was often wet and needed to dry out before stowage. Bruce devised a system of attaching sails to the toe rail with bungee cords so they would be handy, but out of the way when not in use Then there were lines for the various sails on deck, hopefully coiled, but not always.

Our life raft, permanently stored in a hard plastic case, was designed to inflate with a pull of a cord. It's one of those expensive investments you never hope to use. It was kept handy on top of the cabin, and the eight-foot dinghy was lashed over that, together with its oars. Our two solar panels were lashed down on top of the dinghy. The overturned dinghy also covered the midship hatch and in calm weather allowed us to open the hatch to let in fresh air without getting sea-sprayed. In the cockpit, spare five-gallon water jugs were tied behind the tiller. On the aft deck, four ten-pound capacity propane tanks were attached to the port and starboard railings.

Almost every day, laundry hung out to dry, adding to the clutter. Offshore sailing vessels are rarely tidy.

One day we discussed our plans to circum-navigate. Bruce said that although much of this trip had been pretty good, circumnavigating the world would have plenty of times where it would be rough, likely as bad as what we experienced early on our trip off the coast of Oregon. For long passages, timing is dictated by the winds and weather. We only had two years for this adventure, unlike some people who were retired or could work in various countries as they went along. Teachers often did this. For family reasons and financial security, we needed to stick to our two-year plan.

Bruce said that since we only had two years, we would have to keep moving and stay on a strict schedule. Much of the two years would be sailing, with only brief stays once we reached land. He asked what I would think of considering this a South Pacific trip. This would give us time at each place to really enjoy each country and its culture. What a grand idea! Sea life wasn't the goal as far as I was concerned; it was making landfalls. Bruce felt the same. With that in mind, and considering wind patterns, we decided that this trip would be 14 months, rather than two years. It was a great plan and we never regretted changing our goal.

We hadn't seen another living soul since shortly after we left San Diego. Two weeks became three, then four. It was as though we were the world's only inhabitants. That kind of aloneness bothers some people, but it didn't bother us. We were content with each other's company and didn't miss interacting with other people.

We did enjoy talking to family members via ham radio, but that was usually only once or twice a week. Otherwise, it was only the two of us, day in and day out.

Unfavorable winds during the early days of this leg of the journey made the passage longer than we expected and by the end of it, we were anxious to reach landfall. Our supplies were fine, everything on the boat worked as it should and we were both healthy and fit. But it would be wonderful to touch land again and see new and different sights.

Amazingly, our oranges and apples had lasted in good shape for this entire passage, even during the hot weather. The fruit was stored in wooden crates under the dinette in the cabin, away from the direct sun, but often it was hot in the cabin. We lost one orange due to mold, and the apples weren't as crisp as they'd been at first. Otherwise, our light chlorine bath had done the trick to rid the fruit of surface bacteria that would cause spoilage. We finished the last of the fresh fruit shortly before reaching the Marguesas.

We were excited when we saw a frigate bird circle overhead. It meant we were close to land! We watched as the big, mostly black bird skimmed the water, dipped into the sea and plucked out a fish, barely getting his wings wet.

On Monday July 24th, like a little kid, I asked Bruce when we would "get there," reach the Marquesas.

"Oh, probably early Wednesday morning."

If that happened, I would be impressed with the exactness of his calculations. Without navigation know-how, you can miss an island by days, going right past it. To cross an ocean with no landmarks, using only the stars and sun for navigation, takes skill.

In any event, I had my sights set on Wednesday. By then we would have been at sea for thirty-five days. I was ready to get there, to set foot on land, take a long walk, and drink something cold. Strangely, I also felt reluctance to again open our lives to others. We'd been in a world of our own and we were comfortable with that.

First landfall, approaching Nuku Hiva

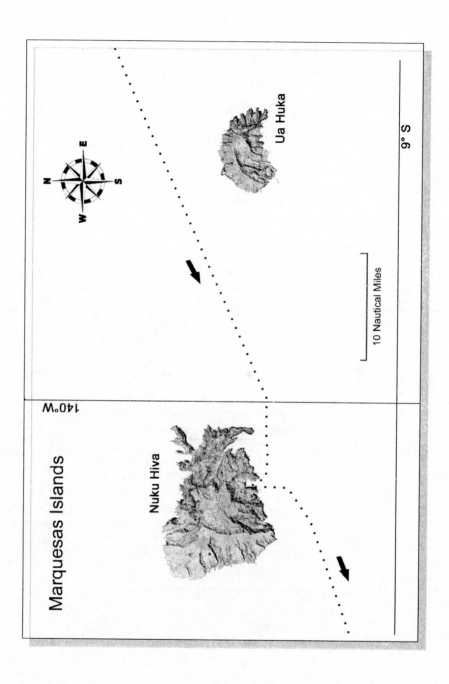

First Landfall – the Marquesas

Log Entry—July 25, 1989: Land Ho! Nuka Hiva off our starboard bow!

*F*rom scraps of the heavy nylon material I'd used to make our storage bags, Bruce had made a French courtesy flag, three stripes of blue, white, and red. The American flag always flew at the stern on the aft leech of our mizzen sail. He now rigged the French courtesy flag from the starboard spreader off the main. Below the courtesy flag he hung a square yellow quarantine flag that he also made, a signal to the harbor authorities inviting them to come aboard to inspect the vessel prior to being cleared or admitted into the country. In most cases, we knew that Bruce would go to them when reaching port, but flying the "Q" quarantine flag was protocol for an arriving vessel until they had cleared customs.

As we approached the Marquesas, from miles away we were aware of the islands' aroma, a tropical arboretum rich with scents of earth tinted with tropical flowers and fruits. We passed north of Ua Nuka before approaching Nuka Hiva, the largest of the twelve Marquesas Islands. As we neared land, dolphins greeted us with wild cavorting around the boat, slicing the water at extraordinary speeds. Our depth sounder was turned on and the dolphins kept setting off the shallow water alarm. We finally turned off the depth sounder since we had plenty of good light to see any obstacles. I stood in the bow, ready to signal Bruce if I saw any coral heads or changes in water color. I had to laugh at the dolphins playful antics as they welcomed us to French Polynesia.

Bruce found a place to anchor among other boats in Taiahoe Bay. The rattling of the anchor chain was a welcome sound as the anchor was lowered 28 feet into the bay. We made it! We hung our boarding ladder and lowered the dinghy so that Bruce could row about 200 yards to shore. As required when first arriving, only the ship's captain goes ashore to the harbor master and customs officials to present the boat's documentation papers and the crew's passports. He carried our important ship's papers in a heavy zippered plastic bag.

Getting to shore was a challenge. The Marquesas aren't surrounded by coral reefs, so ocean swells come right into the bay. Timing a dinghy landing to avoid a breaking wave is pretty tricky, but Bruce managed without getting too wet.

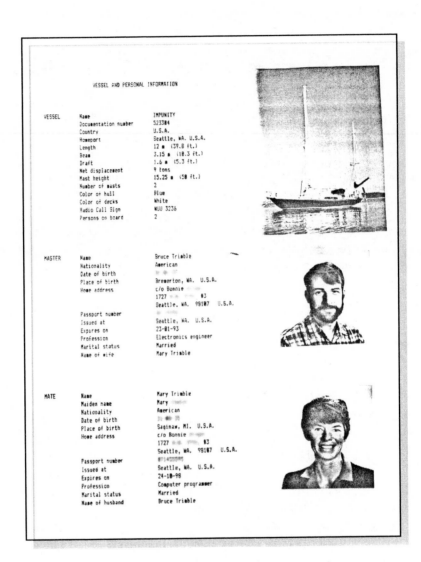

VESSEL AND PERSONAL INFORMATION

VESSEL	Name	IMPUNITY
	Documentation number	52338**4**
	Country	U.S.A.
	Homeport	Seattle, WA. U.S.A.
	Length	12 m (39.8 ft.)
	Beam	3.15 m (10.3 ft.)
	Draft	1.6 m (5.3 ft.)
	Net displacement	9 tons
	Mast height	15.25 m (50 ft.)
	Number of masts	2
	Color of hull	Blue
	Color of decks	White
	Radio Call Sign	WUU 3236
	Persons on board	2

MASTER	Name	Bruce Trimble
	Nationality	American
	Date of birth	
	Place of birth	Bremerton, WA. U.S.A.
	Home address	c/o Bonnie
		1727 #3
		Seattle, WA. 99107 U.S.A.
	Passport number	
	Issued at	Seattle, WA. U.S.A.
	Expires on	23-01-93
	Profession	Electronics engineer
	Marital status	Married
	Name of wife	Mary Trimble

MATE	Name	Mary Trimble
	Maiden name	Mary
	Nationality	American
	Date of birth	
	Place of birth	Saginaw, MI. U.S.A.
	Home address	c/o Bonnie
		1727 #3
		Seattle, WA. 99107 U.S.A.
	Passport number	
	Issued at	Seattle, WA. U.S.A.
	Expires on	24-10-98
	Profession	Computer programmer
	Marital status	Married
	Name of husband	Bruce Trimble

Document we used to help clear customs

I couldn't wait to touch ground, but busied myself tidying up the boat, restoring the midship bunk back to a settee, taking a quick bucket bath and getting fully dressed for the first time in weeks. The anchorage was a bit rough with choppy wave action.

Surprised with how many countries were represented in the harbor, I saw flags on yachts from the United States, Sweden, New Zealand, France, Zambia in South Africa, Germany, plus a French Navy ship.

Bruce was gone the better part of an hour, but returned pleased that our boat and crew's documentation in French had made registration easier. He came back with instructions for the next required entry steps we were to take, but this time we could do them together.

We boarded the dinghy and negotiated a splashy landing, pulling the dinghy up on the sandy beach so it wouldn't get washed back to sea. There was no boaters' dock. I took a few wobbly steps until I got used to walking on steady ground.

Our first order of business was to post personal bonds. People arriving in private yachts were required to post a bond for each person aboard, amounting to $1,700 for the two of us for the duration of our stay in French Polynesia. From our research, we already knew this was a requirement, but many yachtsmen were caught off guard. Some objected, loudly. Some sailors seem to feel that since the wind is free, everything else should be, too. I understood the reasoning behind the bond. In French Polynesia, it isn't uncommon to wreck a boat on coral reefs. The government here has been stuck with that clean-up, even having to give sailors money to fly home. There's no reason the local government should bear that obligation, so the bond money is enough to at least send someone home, plus help defray cleanup costs. Other than a small service fee, the full amount would be returned when we left our final French Polynesian port.

We had money set aside and went to the island's only bank to purchase our bonds. The friendly bank official sat behind a desk. There were no tellers or tellers' cages, or even a counter, only the one fellow at his desk. The money was kept in a regular desk drawer, not even separated by dividers. Everything was done by hand, though he had a calculator. He accepted our American currency and issued a bond receipt.

Our next required stop was to surrender our weapons at the police department, more property called *gendarme*, since French was the official language. We had brought our weapons on our journey in case we should be accosted by pirates at sea, a very real concern. Before relinquishing them to the local authorities, Bruce had put trigger locks on both our handguns, his Ruger .357 Magnum and my Smith & Wesson .38 Special. We had been warned to lock the triggers so they couldn't be used by others. The law is that visitors leave the country with the exact weapons and ammunition they had when entering. We found the *gendarme*, a Marquesan, helpful and friendly. He admired our guns and said French weapons lacked accuracy. He spoke a little English and explained that with a French gun you aim here (he pointed) but it shoots there (he pointed in a different direction). We were given a carbon copy of the form we had signed surrendering our guns and about 100 rounds of ammunition.

Our business complete, we set out to explore our first foreign port of call. It seemed hotter on land than at sea, but the gentle breeze helped keep us comfortable. Taiahoe Bay is surrounded on three sides by mountains 2,000 to 3,000 feet high with peaks up to 4,000 feet. The area is lush with myriad green foliage. The people, reserved and dignified, didn't make a fuss over us, which was a relief. The limited grocery selection was disappointing, but we really didn't need much. We'd barely made a dent in our supplies. We were mostly hungry for fresh bread, fruit and vegetables. We found some finger bananas and pamplemousse, a fibrous fruit that looks like a grape-fruit but tastes more like sweet lime.

Ancient Marquesan tikis

The grocery stores were small and carried French or English brands. We were glad we had our own supplies. The local fare was expensive. For a small can of tuna, $7; for a single 12-ounce bottle of beer, $8; a faded box of cereal two years past the pull-date, $5. One thing I would do differently when provisioning would be to buy several pint jars of mayonnaise rather than the quart size. Without refrigeration, mayonnaise will spoil once the jar is opened. We splurged on a small jar for $3.50.

Joy of joys, by following our noses we found a bakery and delicious French bread for thirty-five cents a loaf! Another small variety store carried supplies including cold drinks. A Coke never tasted so good. It was the first cold thing we'd had for seven weeks.

While in that small variety store, we met three yachtsmen, each from separate boats. One, a German fellow, could easily have passed for a pirate. He seemed friendly enough but was a big man and looked pretty tough, He had a scraggly beard and his clothes were a mess.

One of the first things we did when we returned to the boat was to put up the awning. What a blessing it was. The awning shaded the cockpit from the hot sun and even made a difference below decks. As the sun lowered, we unrolled the awning's sides to maintain shade.

Now that we no longer bobbed around, coffee tasted good again and at the store I'd found the European NesCafé, so different from the type available in the States. I first had it in Africa and was so disappointed when we returned to the U.S. to find an entirely different NesCafé product. But here was the "good stuff" again! I've never figured out why the two taste so different. I knew that the European Nes-

Café had limited shelf life. Perhaps the lack of pre-servatives made the difference in taste.

Preparing dinner was actually fun with a galley that held still. Finally, I could use two hands to prepare a meal

After 35 days at sea, Bruce and I could finally sleep together for a full night. What a treat!

The next day, before we left to explore the island, a fellow in a dinghy motored up to us. At my lack of recognition, he smiled. "I am Claudius. I have shaved and cleaned up," he said in a heavy German accent. The pirate! "I would like to invite you for coffee this afternoon." He indicated his boat, a nice craft anchored close to us. We gladly accepted his invitation and agreed we would be there by 3:00.

We again faced a rough landing when we took the dinghy ashore. The hem of my shorts got wet, but dried quickly in the heat.

We didn't linger on the beach because of stinging sandflies. We heard of some people having nasty infections from the bites. After beaching the dinghy, we hurried across the black sand to the road, carrying a full laundry bag.

At the small variety store the previous day we'd learned of a woman who did laundry for a reasonable price. I could easily keep up with our daily clothes and galley towels, but it was wonderful to have sheets, bath towels and that day's clothes washed for us. When we picked up the laundry the next day, it was clean and nicely folded. It was worth every penny. I noticed most of her business consisted of huge piles of clothes. I gathered that most people didn't do laundry at sea.

After we dropped off our laundry, we explored Nuka Hiva. The main road followed the beach, separated only by towering palm trees. The road, paved with light colored asphalt, had crushed coral and shells for filler, rather than gravel. Other small dirt roads meandered off from the main one. Very few cars were on the road. We saw a couple of trucks, but mostly bicyclists or walkers.

Making our way out of the market area, we passed green pastures. We noticed a number of small horses, not ponies nor miniatures, just small animals. We wondered if in-breeding caused their diminutive size. The goats and sheep looked small, too. Normal-sized chickens roamed freely.

Before missionaries converted the people to Christianity, the Marquesans fought among themselves and were noted cannibals, but diseases brought by the white man had a more devastating effect on the population than earlier practices had. For 40 years, the Marquesas were ravaged by whalers, traders, and slave buyers. Finally, the Marquesan chiefs asked France to help and a treaty was signed in 1842. To this day, the Marquesas Islands are under French administrative autonomy.

We walked to a beautiful Catholic church, Notre Dame Cathedral, surrounded by lush, immaculate grounds, rich with a variety of greens interspersed with brilliant red and yellow hibiscus and many flowers I couldn't identify. The stone church had exquisitely carved wooden doors, probably ten feet tall.

Climbing a hill, we found a flat landing with two large stone tiki carvings, about eight-feet tall. We were impressed with the detail. The Marquesas Islands are known for their stone and wood tikis.

It felt so good to walk at our leisure and not have a schedule to keep. As we made our way back to the boat, we stopped for a cold Coke for me, a cold beer for Bruce, and more French bread, still warm from the oven.

At 3:00 we rowed to Claudius' boat, *Pegasus*, a beautiful well-kept craft a little larger than *Impunity*. We brought a gift of our dried fruit and he was grateful, saying he would save it to eat at sea. Much to my amazement, he served coffee in china cups. He mentioned his mother entertained a lot and he often acted as her host. He often sailed single-handed, but sometimes had a mate. At this time he was alone.

Claudius was an experienced sailor. From the minute we stepped on board it was obvious that he'd be capable of handling pretty much anything on a boat. The center cockpit was rigged so that a single person on board could handle the sails.

As Claudius poured more of his good strong coffee into our dainty cups he asked, "Who does the cooking?" He spoke grammatically perfect English, but had a strong German accent. I told him I did and about all of our preparation and supplies. He was impressed. "Tell me what you cook while at sea." I named several dishes and he nodded in appreciation. "You have the hardest job. What we do is easy compared to that."

After seeing how hard Bruce worked, I doubted that, but it was good to hear anyway.

"Do you know," he continued, "most people don't cook like that at sea?" No, I hadn't known. I figured everyone did what I did. "Ask around. You will be surprised."

As we became acquainted with other sailors, I learned Claudius was right. Many of the people we met rarely cooked at sea. One couple said they cooked a pot of rice every few days, stood in the galley and ate it right out of the pot. Another woman told me all they have at sea were salty snacks. "You can't cook in those rough seas," she insisted. I didn't tell her I did.

94

Another couple we knew said that they had planned to cook, but the woman got so seasick all she could do was lie down while he was stuck with the boat's operation. They ate crackers and canned fruit. Another woman said she only fixed sandwiches, using crackers when the bread ran out.

We found the biggest complaint of things gone wrong at sea was failing refrigerators. Many refrigeration systems can't take the rough jostling at sea and often leak refrigerants or their compressors fail. Most boat refrigerator motors only work when the engine is running so if the engine fails, there is no refrigeration. Boat after boat came in with spoiled food, or very little food because they'd had to dump their rotten perishables overboard. People whose boats had refrigeration and freezers had planned their food accordingly, and when their systems failed, they were at a loss for food and then forced to buy groceries at the exorbitant local prices.

We were glad *Impunity*'s previous owner had thrown the refrigerator overboard. Without a refrigerator or freezer our lives were much simpler.

Many inexperienced cruisers didn't realize how essential it is to thoroughly seal items in heavy plastic, heat-sealed bags. Resealable zipper storage bags don't work on a rough passage—the zipper commonly fails and the contents leak out, or moisture leaks in. In one case, they had stored fresh fruit and vegetables in zipper storage bags below decks, thinking it was the coldest place. Once in tropical seas, their boat reeked of rotting food.

Another common complaint from boaters just arriving was green water in their fresh-water tanks. They hadn't treated their water tank before they left and in the tropical heat algae had grown profusely. I saw one sample and their water was green as a lime popsicle. Adding a tiny bit of chlorine bleach when the tank is filled will keep that from happening. It's such an easy solution. Each time Bruce put fresh water in the tank, he added a small quantity of bleach. We couldn't taste it, and we never had green water.

We invited Claudius for dinner one night and I served vegetarian spaghetti made with our Washington State University Creamery canned cheese. He loved it and I sent the leftovers home with him. I had learned to make that in Africa where meat was often scarce. Many of our "survival" skills we'd learned the hard way when we served with the Peace Corps in The Gambia, West Africa.

In port, we couldn't use the ham radio since Bruce didn't have a local license. We were anxious to call home to let our family know we had arrived safely. The only phone available to us was at the post office, but it had odd hours: early morning, then closed mid-day for an hour or two, then open until late afternoon or early evening, depending on the day of the week. Since there was a two and a half-hour time difference between the Marquesas and Seattle, it was hard to find a time when the family would be home and the post office open. We finally got through. It was always good to make contact with family.

Bruce and I agreed that we would keep his mechanical and electronic skills quiet. Boats often came limping into port and he didn't want to spend his time working on other people's boats. We met a nice couple ashore and invited them aboard our boat. He asked Bruce what kind of engine we had and Bruce told him a Yanmar diesel, 3 cylinder, 25 horsepower. The fellow's eyes lit up. "So do we!" But he went on to say they were having some problems with it and he was hesitant to go back to sea with the engine not working properly.

Bruce broke his own rule and said he'd have a look at it. We all rowed over to their boat and Bruce found the problem. They were so grateful, they offered to take us out to dinner. They suggested we go up the hill to an inn run by an American couple. The restaurant didn't have a menu; guests ate whatever the cook found available. We were served lobster, followed by chicken and salad, with flan for dessert. It was a delightful treat for us.

While we enjoyed a lovely meal, our new friends told us about an incident that happened to them while anchored in a bay in Mexico. They had spent an evening visiting on a neighboring boat. Just going from their boat to the other boat in their dinghy, they hadn't taken their shoes, purse or his wallet since they wouldn't need those items unless they went ashore. They'd had a nice evening playing cards and then, much later, they climbed into their dinghy to return to their own boat. It was dark, but they soon realized their sailboat was gone!

Panicked, they went back to their friend's boat and spent the rest of the night there. First thing in the morning, they went ashore and reported the missing boat. They didn't know if it had been stolen, became untied, or dragged anchor, so it was unknown if a crime had been committed.

With no money, no identification, not even shoes, they were in a terrible situation. To their surprise and relief, an American, a man they didn't know, gave them $500 so they could buy shoes and stay in a hotel until they could receive money from home. No strings attached, he simply wanted to help stranded strangers. (They got his name and address and were able to pay him back.)

Mexican officials put out notices and the couple talked to fishermen and anyone going to sea. Finally, about two weeks after it "went missing" the boat was spotted. The fishermen who saw it said it was merely bobbing along, laundry still hanging in the transom, anchor hanging on its chain in the deep water. It didn't appear to be damaged. After observing the boat for some time to make sure no one was aboard, the fishermen motored over to it and one climbed aboard, got the engine running, weighed anchor, and brought it back. Everything was intact, even her purse and their wallets were still there.

The couple still sailed that boat, so thankful for the kindness of others. "And now you've fixed the engine for us. We can't thank you enough."

When it rains in the tropics, it can be a real downpour, sometimes two or three inches in an hour. Then, it suddenly stops and the sun shines, drying everything off. Now that we had the awning up, Bruce was able to try out the rain-catching system he'd designed. He'd let the awning rinse off for a minute or two, then loosen a halyard to allow the top to sag, and hoses would direct the water into five-gallon jugs. It worked beautifully.

Many people relied on water available close to shore. Brown, pebbly water came out of the spigot and sailors were hesitant to put it in their water tanks. They had to let it sit and wait for the mud to settle, but it was never what I'd call clean water. It was a huge problem. You can't manage without fresh water.

Typical of boaters, we traded magazines and books. We looked forward to having a whole new crop of reading material.

A couple of days before we were to leave, we decided to fill the propane tank we'd used at sea. We inquired where we might buy propane, but were told that only butane was available. Bruce said he was sure butane would work. A fellow at the variety store asked us to go with him to a place on the beach where a large butane tank hung from a high tree branch. He connected our small 10-pound tank and filled it by gravity. Every once in awhile, he'd loosen a value to let air escape. It took a long time and would not fill as full as it would have under pressure, but it gave us security knowing we had a better supply.

It was hard to believe, but we had been in the Marquesas for two weeks. It was time to move on.

On our last Friday night in Taiahoe Bay, we went back to the inn where we'd gone as guests. By this time we'd met several yachties and seven of us enjoyed the meal together, a couple from Boston, a couple from Aspen, Colorado and our German friend, Claudius. Most of us were leaving, so it was a farewell dinner to each other and to the Marquesas.

The next morning we went ashore for what we thought would be the last time. Bruce and I took our small backpacks to carry several loaves of French bread, fruit and our weapons back to the boat. The first order of business was the weapons. For some reason, we both dreaded this, but we walked the distance to the *gendarme* station and presented our receipt to the same fellow who had originally taken our guns. His dark face colored as he said, "Yes, well, the Commissioner would like to talk to you."

"Is there something wrong?" Bruce asked.

"Oh, no, no. But before I can give you your weapons, the Commissioner has asked to see you."

Oh boy, what was this all about? We followed his directions to a big pink concrete building, the Commissioner's residence and office. We were escorted to a large bare room with only a wooden desk in the middle and a chair behind the desk, where the Commissioner sat, and two wooden chairs in front of the desk. A huge ceiling fan slowly rotated above his desk. Tall, shuttered windows lined the outside wall. For some reason, the movie *Casablanca* popped into my mind. The Commissioner rose, warmly greeted us and invited us to sit.

He could speak very little English and what little he could was difficult to understand. After saying what we supposed was something to the effect he hoped our visit there had been satisfactory, he came to the business at hand. Leaning forward and folding his hands, looking at Bruce, he said, "I want to sell your small gun."

I looked at Bruce's furrowed brow. He didn't understand, either.

"Oh!" I said, the Commissioner's meaning dawning on me. "You want to buy the Smith & Wesson."

"Yes, yes! That's it. I want to buy that gun."

In the first place, what he asked was illegal. I'm sure that's why the *gendarme* looked so embarrassed. The law dictated we leave with the exact number of weapons and ammunition with which we arrived. Now the top official on the island was asking us to do something illegal?

In the second place, that was my handgun, a gift from Bruce, and I didn't want to part with it. My mind whirled. I glanced at Bruce. He was thunderstruck.

"But you see," I said, gesturing to Bruce, "my husband gave that gun to me for Christmas. I cannot part with it." I looked lovingly at Bruce.

The Commissioner was quick to respond. "Oh, but of course. It was a gift from your husband. I do understand." His manner was gracious and he seemed to completely agree with our position.

The Commissioner stood and shook our hands. "Enjoy the rest of your journey." At least that's pretty much what it sounded like.

In a daze, we left and walked back to the police station to pick up our weapons. Bruce squeezed my hand. "Mary, that was brilliant, calling on the French sense of romance. I was so stunned I was speechless."

As we entered the station the *gendarme* was just hanging up the phone. He looked relieved. "I am so sorry," he said, shaking his head in apology. "Let me get your weapons." He asked Bruce to inspect them and then sign a receipt. We turned to leave, but he stopped us.

"Please come this way."

No! Now what? My heart pounded. I glanced at Bruce's narrowed eyes. He took my arm as we followed the fellow toward the back of the station and entered an empty jail. Bruce's hand on my arm gripped tighter.

"Here we are," the *gendarme* said, as he opened the door to a sunny yard. "I want to give you this pamplemousse for your journey." We stepped into what was his back yard; his home was on the other side of the property. Branches of two trees sagged with the heavy fruit. He began picking fruit and handing them to us. First one, then two, then he continued until our arms were full of the fruit. Each time we protested that it was enough, he would say, "No, please take it." Bruce knelt and put them in our packs, filling them to the brim. We realized that it was the *gendarme's* way of apology for our inconvenience.

We left in good spirits and could see the *gendarme's* relief. Our packs were so full of fruit and weapons, we had to row the dinghy back to the boat, unload, then go back to shore for our last-minute shopping.

At 7:30 the next morning we weighed anchor and were on our way to Tahiti with plenty of fruit on hand.

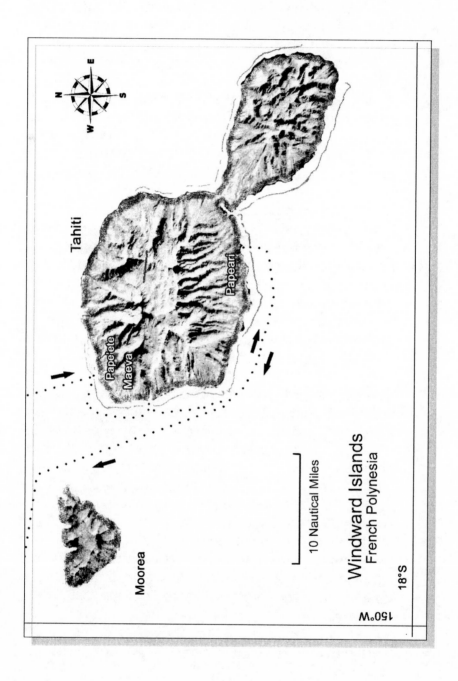

Windward Islands
French Polynesia

10 Nautical Miles

Tahiti

Papeari

Papeete
Maeva

Moorea

18°S

150°W

Our Private Bay – Tahiti

Log Entry—August 16, 1989: We are suspended in space.

We left the Marquesas August 8, shortly before eight in the morning. A pot of turkey vegetable soup sat snugly between pot restraints on the gently rocking gimbaled stove, airtight in the pressure cooker.

We cleared the west end of Tuamotus Islands and their coral reef hazards. Moderate seas and favorable 25- to 30-knot easterly winds kept our speed at 6 knots. The leg to Tahiti would be 800 miles, roughly a week's passage.

Although others who had been anchored with us planned to leave about the same time, we hadn't seen a soul since leaving the Marquesas. It was always amazing to me how quickly one becomes alone at sea.

The next evening after the Maritime Mobile Net, we patched a call to son Jeff and wished him a belated happy birthday, which actually fell on our departure day. The next day we called daughter Robin. We rotated through the family so that everyone eventually heard from us on that passage.

After three days of good sailing, the wind dropped and we were becalmed for almost three days. Any progress we made was mostly because we ran the engine. During that time, for two nights, we experienced a strange phenomenon with water so calm and smooth that the stars' reflection was as clearly visible as those in the sky. It gave us a feeling of being suspended in space, with stars above, below, and all around us. It was magical, and eerie.

While becalmed, it was very hot with no relief, though cooler at night. The wind picked up and we scooted along, but were slowed by a couple of squalls. Nearing Tahiti, we needed to be extra alert as ship traffic picked up. The passage was delightful, with enough activity to keep us busy, but not frantic. We were happy mariners.

During the passage from San Diego, we'd learned how to keep fresh vegetables a little longer by placing them in a plastic tub covered with a wet towel, allowing condensation to keep it cool. During the day, we moved the tub around to keep it in shade and in a breeze, when possible.

Once out of the doldrums we made pretty good time. Even on the slow days, we easily fell into our routine and enjoyed the journey.

Radio Tahiti crackled to life with a mixture of Polynesian, French and American music. We navigated around the late actor Marlon Brando's island of Tetiaroa.

At two in the afternoon, after nine days at sea, we entered Papeete Harbor. As we expected, there were many boats in the harbor, but we hoped to put up with the crowded conditions for only two or three days. Papeete's mooring dock was full of private yachts, but we were glad to anchor out and avoid the noise and crowds. Anchoring out was free, but tying up at the dock cost money.

Unlike other landfalls, Papeete has an unusual moorage system, appropriately called "Tahitian style." Rather than piers protruding over the water, Papeete has a concrete dock that runs along the edge of the water, parallel to the beach. To moor Tahitian style, rather than go in bow first, a yachtsman drops one or two anchors from the bow into the bay, turns the boat and backs up toward the dock, then ties a line or two to cleats on shore. It can be a tricky maneuver getting a boat turned around to go in stern first. Once moored, boaters often put a plank from their stern to the pier for access on and off their boats.

After Bruce cleared *Impunity* through customs, we walked Papeete's streets. It was fun seeing it for the first time, but the city wasn't for us. Papeete was noisy with heavy traffic and honking horns. It was difficult to stay on any kind of sidewalk. We would suddenly find ourselves in the street when the sidewalk ended or abruptly shifted over a few feet, or we'd find a car parked right in the middle of the walkway.

We're not strollers, so for people like us who like to clip right along, this was frustrating.

However, the marvelous Papeete open-air market had rows and rows of produce beautifully displayed and reasonably priced. We found meat a bit pricey, but we bought a couple of pork chops, a pineapple, tomatoes, and cabbage.

Open market in Papeete

The waters surrounding Tahiti are filled with coral reefs, so we stopped at a government office for a detailed chart. French charts can be annoying since they often don't adhere to navigation *Rules of the Road*, which is accepted by the rest of the world.

Some French charts used Paris as the starting point for measuring longitude, rather than Greenwich, England that standard charts use. This difference affects longitude, which matters when plotting a position. Also, the French reversed the "red right returning" rule which to the rest of the world means that when returning to port the red channel markers should stay to the navigator's right. In addition, we found that aids to navigation were not always maintained. Coming into a small harbor, the buoys or markers shown on the chart might or might not actually be there.

We checked in at the post office and found we had a couple of letters, but we were expecting more since this was our first mail-call since the trip began. We had left a list of general delivery addresses with family and friends for the next four landfalls. Our Tahiti "address" was:

Bruce and Mary Trimble
Yacht *Impunity*
Poste Restante
Papeete, Tahiti
French Polynesia

In addition, we suggested they write "Hold for yacht in transit." Apparently something wasn't working because various family members had mentioned when we'd talked to them via ham radio that they'd mailed us letters. We treasured the two we'd received, but were disappointed that the others hadn't caught up with us.

Because algae tends to grow in diesel, particularly in warm weather, Bruce bought a good biocide to add to the fuel tank. We'd heard of a few boats having engine trouble due to algae clogging fuel filters, and he wanted to head off fuel problems before they got started. It was expensive, especially in French Polynesia, but we felt the precaution worth the cost.

After a couple of days, we'd had about all we could stand of Papeete with its noise and congestion. We craved a quiet, restful moorage.

The fuel tank on *Impunity* didn't have a gauge, but Bruce could measure the level with a marked stick. We motored to the fuel dock, and waited in line three and a half hours before taking on 108 liters of diesel. While we waited, hot and miserable, we assured ourselves that leaving this teeming mass of inefficiency was absolutely the right thing to do. We couldn't wait to get out of Papeete.

After working our way out of the Papeete Harbor, we sailed in a stiff breeze five miles southwest to Maeva Beach and dropped anchor in 50 feet of water.

Outrigger at sunset

About 40 boats anchored with us, but without the city noises it seemed calmer. We saw a few yachts from Seattle, but didn't get acquainted with any of them. With this many boats around, we knew Maeva Beach was only a temporary anchorage for us.

Long outrigger canoes, some 6-man, some 12-man, glided past the anchorage in the early evenings, often to the rhythm of the paddlers' chanting. Outrigger races are popular in Polynesia and both men and women teams participate in this vigorous inter-island sport. They were thrilling to watch, especially against a setting sun.

Rowing 300 feet to shore in our dinghy, we walked through the dusty streets of a little shanty town. It was pleasant after the hustle and bustle of Papeete. Rather than cars honking we heard pigs snuffling, chickens cackling and lots of barking dogs. We stopped at a grocery store and bought a sausage to use on a pizza.

Later, as our pizza baked, a rank odor wafted from our oven. By the time the pizza was done, neither of us could eat it. That sausage must have been well past the due date. I opened a couple cans of chili for dinner, disgusted we had wasted time, propane, money, and ingredients on something inedible.

In Fodor's *South Pacific* guidebook we learned of the Lagoonarium that was within walking distance. We again rowed ashore and tied the dinghy to a rickety pier. Walking to the Lagoonarium was a bit of a trek, but very worthwhile. The aquarium is built under a section of coral reef, so we were actually under water and looking at fish in their own habitat. After the heat of the walk, it felt good to be in the cool underwater atmosphere. The Lagoonarium was a photographers paradise and Bruce took full advantage of it.

The south coast of Tahiti was known to be rather isolated and sounded more to our liking. We weighed anchor from Maeva Beach at 5:15 in the morning and by 6:00 were outside the reef. Strong trade winds forced us to reduce sail, then suddenly we were in the wind shadow behind the island and had to drop the sails and turn on the engine. Coming around the south end of the island, the trades were strong again and coming straight at us. We knew that to get to the anchorage at Papieri on the south side of Tahiti, we'd have to navigate through narrow channels and a coral reef, so we motored to make better time, rather than tacking back and forth under sail. For good visibility we wanted to have the sun high when we reached our destination, Papieri, so that we could spot hazards in the water.

Reefs are under water, often just below the surface. Geologically "older" islands like Tahiti have a barrier reef surrounding them with only small gaps where boats can pass through. Between these gaps, the water may only be two to eight feet deep over the reef. Because trade winds generally blow in the same direction, water washes over the reef on the windward (upwind) side of the island, and rushes out through gaps in the reef on the leeward (downwind) side. Taking a boat through a gap in a reef means dealing with a strong four- to six-knot current.

Bruce's insistence on having good light when crossing a reef was important here. With heart pounding, I stood at the bow with Bruce at the helm, watching for signals from me on which way to turn.

As we approached the windward side of Papieri from the open sea going three to four knots, huge swells passed under *Impunity*, then crashed on the reef. But we could also see a stretch of smoother water marking the pass through the reef. We knew we had to be on exactly the right track through the correct gap in the reef. With the current pushing us along, there was no turning back; we were committed. Bruce lined the boat up with the reef's opening and we shot through the gap at a combined ten or so knots gained from our speed plus the current's speed.

During the 14 months we cruised the South Pacific, we personally knew of five boats that were lost or severely damaged due to running up on a reef.

Once in the lagoon, we wove our way between the channel markers, keeping our eyes on the shallow coral heads disturbingly close on either side of the boat. Soon the bay opened up wide, and we breathed easier.

Only one other boat was in the bay. Lo and behold, it was the *Genesis*, the 30-foot sailboat that had been in the Kenmore marina, in Washington, the very boat our friends had told us to look for. We surprised them when we motored alongside and waved to the fellow on deck and said, "Bill and Alice from Kenmore send their greetings!" His amazed look made us laugh.

We found a spot a good distance from the *Genesis* to drop anchor. How delightful, only two boats in the bay. No worries about swinging into each other, or about hooking each other's anchor chain, always a worry in crowded anchorages.

Greg and Kathy would be our only neighbors for one glorious month. We had just settled in when Greg rowed over in his dinghy and invited us for coffee and pineapple scones.

Aboard *Genesis*, we learned that Greg and Kathy had lived at the Kenmore Marina about a year before we had, and since then had sailed to several French

Polynesian islands, Cook Islands, and New Zealand, where they spent the hurricane season. They sailed back to Papieri where they planned to stay a few months before sailing to Hawaii and then home to Seattle. They had both worked at a Seattle post office and had lived only a few blocks from us in the north end of the city. Small world.

Kathy and Greg had taken French lessons for a year at a Seattle community college so they were well equipped to handle themselves among the French-speaking Tahitians. They had made friends with a local family and could easily converse with them.

It was hard to imagine why this place wasn't well-known as an anchorage. Officially, the area was called Botanical Gardens and once a day in the late afternoon a busload of tourists came to stroll among the gardens, visit the Paul Gauguin Museum, and perhaps enjoy a meal at the small restaurant in the complex. Otherwise, we had the place to ourselves. It was unreal.

Bruce put up the awning, and with an almost constant breeze we stayed cool and comfortable.

We often rowed our dinghy the 200 feet to shore and strolled among the colorful gardens and perfectly trimmed lawns. A gentle stream with multi-colored water lilies gurgled its way through one end of the gardens. Small frangipani trees, sometimes called plumiera, were in bloom. Brilliant white tiare Tahiti, the flower Polynesians often used in leis, contrasted against glossy dark green leaves. I loved their peachy scent. Hibiscus grew in abundance in shades of fuchsia, orange, and blue. We couldn't get over the peace and quiet. Our souls absorbed the serenity.

At one time we had talked about spending time at Moorea Island, visible from Papeete, but now we knew better. Moorea was a popular boaters' destination and would be crowded. No thanks. We were content right here in this paradise off the beaten path.

Amazingly, we hadn't been swimming since we started this journey. You might think cruisers would simply take a dive off their boat, but that's a dangerous thing to do, even on a calm day. A sudden gust of wind can quickly push the boat away. We decided we wouldn't take that kind of risk. In the Marquesas we didn't feel like swimming in the choppy anchorage and, because of the stinging sandflies did not linger on the beach.

For surface swimming and shallow diving to view colorful tropical fish, we had masks, fins and snorkels. I began an impressive shell collection at Papieri. The water temperature was perfect for swimming, just cool enough to be refreshing.

The clean black sand beach lined with palm trees was beautiful. An outdoor shower on the beach was a treat. It was out in the open, so we kept our swimsuits on, but we really didn't need to—no one ever came by when we showered.

On August 31 we celebrated my birthday by rowing our dinghy ashore, then going to the Paul Gauguin Museum. The artist lived in Tahiti for several years in the 1890s and a museum with his works was a popular feature at the Botanical Gardens. We enjoyed strolling through the small gallery and Bruce took a picture of a painting. We topped off the evening with a fish dinner at the cozy but pricey Gauguin restaurant.

The Botanical Gardens had a small, local artisans gift shop and one day we stopped in and found a beautiful oblong bowl, made of coconut wood, 27 inches long, four inches deep, and almost eight inches wide. We wanted to get at least one high-end souvenir from this trip, but this bowl cost $70, which we felt was a little steep. We decided to wait.

We took "le truck," Tahiti's term for a small bus, to Papeete to check for mail and stop at the open-air market. The ride took a little more than an hour. Again, Papeete was fun to visit, but we were so glad to be away from its noisy crowds.

We stopped at the post office to mail our letters and inquire about mail. Only one letter. Bruce had an inspiration. In his limited French he asked the clerk to check under "B" for Bruce and "M" for Mary, and "I" for *Impunity*, in addition to "T" for Trimble. The clerk wasn't very happy with his request, but she found six more letters.

At two Papeete gift shops we found our same coconut wooden bowl for $200. The $70 bowl at the Botanical Gardens' gift store was suddenly a bargain.

Although we visited with Greg and Kathy, we took care to give them space, as they gave us. They often left to visit their Tahitian friends ashore, a family that had sort of adopted them.

Only on two occasions did other boats come to that bay, both in the evening, but they were gone early the next morning. Could they not see what a treasure we had here?

One day Greg, Bruce and I hiked up to a waterfall. It was a strenuous hike with lots of streams to ford. We grew weary of taking tennis shoes off and on, so began crossing with our shoes on, which made for squishy walking. Once at the falls we stepped underneath and enjoyed cooling off with the cascading water pouring over us, clothes and all. It was fun, but we were hot and ready for a swim when we returned to our boats.

As I floated on my back near our boat, I looked up at our tall mast and thought, this is like a dream. I can hardly believe we're doing this and that we have this paradise almost to ourselves. It was a thrill to look out at the expansive sea from our calm anchorage, to see waves breaking on the reef, to look toward land and see rolling green hills, and palm trees swaying in the breeze. All that, and we had the Botanical Gardens to stroll in. It couldn't have been more perfect.

Occasionally we walked down the street about a half-mile to a little grocery store run by a Chinese family. In addition to canned goods, sugar and flour, they carried locally grown fresh fruit and vegetables and good French bread. We could buy jugs of Tahitian wine that was quite decent. We often spoke at length with Lillian, the daughter of the store owners. She was born in Hong Kong but was on a summer break from San Francisco State University. She invited us to go on a drive with her so that we could see more of the island.

The next morning, Sunday, when the store was closed, Lillian picked us up at the Botanical Gardens in her parents' car. We wound uphill on a road leading to the island of Tahiti-iti, which is connected to the big island of Tahiti by a long, narrow strip of land. The view of the reefs and tropical mountains was spectacular. We drove through the peaceful countryside where we saw modest homes with beautiful, lush tropical gardens. It was delightful to cover so much ground in a private car.

Even after 200 years of white man's influence, the Tahitian and Polynesian culture is very much alive. Driving around the island, it became obvious what attracted writers and artists such as Robert Louis Stevenson, Jack London, Somerset Maugham, Paul Gauguin and Henry Adams. Each, in his own way, tried to capture Tahiti's essence and charm.

We invited Lillian for dinner the next Sunday. That was her first time on a live-aboard boat and she marveled at the size of it. I served cheese souffle and a salad and she was surprised we could fix such complete meals on a boat, especially without refrigeration.

Meeting local people made our travels richer. Again, we were glad we'd changed to "Plan B" and had the leisure to do this, rather than keep a hectic sailing schedule to circumnavigate the world.

Greg and Kathy extended an invitation to us from their local Tahitian family. The family lived within walking distance in a nice, small residential neighborhood where all the houses looked pretty much alike: white, cement block with a corrugated roof. The beauty of this home was its garden with brilliant red and yellow flowers, and several fruit trees including a banana tree drooping with fruit. It was interesting to enter a local house, which was plainly furnished, but very tidy, and visit Irene, the mother, William, the father, and three children, a son and two daughters. Irene served chilled glasses of guava juice and little cakes.

They spoke very little English, but Greg and Kathy interpreted for us. We took gifts for the family. We'd bought a few inflatable globes so that we could show people where we lived. The children spent a long time looking where they lived and where we lived, remarking, "You have come so far!" We gave Irene a packet of needles and William a "made in USA" stainless steel fishing knife. In thanking us, they all kissed us on both cheeks. Bruce remarked later that it had been a long time since he'd been kissed by a man, and that had been his father.

Mary viewing Vaipahi Falls near Papeari, Tahiti

The next morning William stopped by with a bunch of green finger bananas, probably 100 or so bananas on a three-foot stalk. He rowed to our boat in his outrigger canoe. I started to take them, but then remembered that there might be bugs and hesitated. "Bugs?" I asked. He dropped the bunch into the sea and when it popped up, he said "No more." He also gave us about a half-dozen papayas from their yard.

We enjoyed the fresh fruit. Of course the bananas all ripened about the same time and one early morning we heard soft plop, plops, as they fell off the stalk onto the deck. That evening we shared a big bowl of banana pudding with Greg and Kathy.

One evening Greg rowed over with the exciting news that William and his son had invited us to go fishing the next morning from their outrigger canoe. As scheduled, William picked us up at 5:30. We paddled in the outrigger for a distance, and then William threw out an anchor about a mile from shore, but on a reef in only about four feet of water. We dropped overboard and snorkeled through a pass in the barrier reef. We swam a distance from the outrigger and were dazzled by the coral and fish in colors from brown and black to bright blues, oranges, and yellows. Some of the fish glowed like neon lights.

We collected large shellfish, which William and Greg immediately cleaned. William made a point of showing us that he was using the knife that we had given him. He had brought fresh limes from his yard and now soaked slices of the just-caught snail meat in the lime juice for about 5 minutes. Then we ate it, raw. I was surprised with how good it was.

William and his son both speared parrotfish and I saw Bruce wince when he noticed William tuck a just-caught fish in his very brief swim suit. They brought the fish back to the outrigger and again gave it the lime treatment. We feasted on raw fish that had been swimming only five minutes before.

On our "down time" Bruce busied himself with preventive maintenance. Our main water tank was a large bladder made of a rubberized fabric. Bruce searched below decks for any possible leaks. He also watched for leaks on fittings throughout the boat. He checked the battery voltage level a couple times a day. On deck, he looked for sail chaffing as the result of rubbing against a shroud. He'd check for worn or frayed lines. He installed new gaskets on the portholes. He sanded and varnished the exposed brightwork on deck.

It often rained for a bit in the afternoon, sometimes long enough for us to collect rain water in our fresh water tank. Unless it was wind-driven rain, we could usually continue to sit in the cockpit under our awning, but occasionally were forced to go below decks.

Greg and Kathy had collected a number of shells ranging from the large spider variety down to tiny augers. We'd collected a few shells too, but were unwilling to put up with the smell and time it takes to clean shells that still have critters residing in them. Greg and Kathy had jewelers' equipment and had professionally polished many of the shells.

Our new friends had been on their trip quite awhile and were running low on food supplies. We made a trade that was favorable to all: some of their shells for some of our canned goods. So with the trade, plus some shells they gave me for my birthday, and with those I'd found, we had the start of a nice collection.

Once, when Greg and Kathy were over for dinner they brought their cassette tapes. The tape deck that came with *Impunity* could record which allowed us to make copies of favorites. We also exchanged reading material.

It was hard to believe, but our month in Tahiti was coming to an end. We prepared our boat for another passage. Bora Bora, here we come!

Greg and Kathy from *Genesis*, paddling William's outrigger canoe

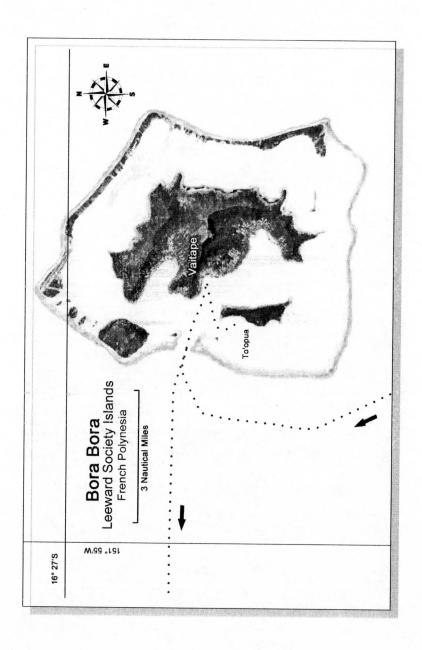

Picture Perfect – Bora Bora

Log Entry—September 26, 1989: Impunity is like a toy sailboat on a smooth pond.

*I*t was hard leaving our Papieri paradise and our friends there. Greg and Kathy invited us aboard the evening before departure for a farewell glass of wine. We hoped to see one another in Seattle.

We dreaded going back through the reef, but had a perfect sunny morning. We carefully threaded our way out, with me scanning the sea from the bow and Bruce at the helm.

In about 30 seconds, we went from flat calm to big ocean swells that had traveled unobstructed for 5,000 miles.The 200-foot wide pass we motored through had huge breakers crashing onto the reef on either side of us. It all happened so fast, our adrenalin pumped double-time.

Suddenly, we were back in the open sea driving fast with favorable southwest trade winds. *Impunity* sliced the water westward along the southern coast of Tahiti. After a few hours, the winds died completely and we motored for about 12 hours, which meant hand-steering. During the night we saw the Island of Moorea silhouetted against the stars.

On a cloudless night, the stars in the South Pacific are crystal clear and bright. Without city lights or dust, they appear bright even close to the horizon. Well south of the equator, we saw no North Star or Big Dipper, but could see the Southern Cross and Magellenic Clouds, a constellation and galaxy of the Milky Way. Orion, familiar to us in the Northwest, can be seen, but appears to be standing on his head.

During my night watch the wind picked up with a purpose and I had to wake Bruce to shut down the engine and help set the sails. For the rest of the night and all the next day we had good sailing, though a bit rough. We scooted past Huahine of the Society Islands and the southern tip of Raiatea, then turned northwest toward Bora Bora.

Raiatea sheltered us from ocean swells, but we had ideal wind. It was a strange sensation. We scooted along like a toy sailboat on a smooth pond, or as Bruce expressed it, as though *Impunity* were on rails. It was the smoothest sailing we'd ever experienced. How perfect was this! Eighty-three degrees, stars all around, perfect winds, no sea swells, no rocking, no splashes, just a gentle heeling at a silent five knots.

From 35 miles away we began seeing the glow of Bora Bora, probably the lights from a hotel on the southern tip of the island. During my watch, Bruce changed our course to give us plenty of sea room to avoid the reef southwest of Bora Bora. By 6:30 a.m. we were in the lagoon and inside the protective barrier reef.

Bora Bora was an independent kingdom until annexed by the French in 1888. During World War II the island served as a supply base for the United States. Military construction included an airstrip and after the war that airstrip would be the only inter-national airport in all of French Polynesia until 1960.

The anchorage at Vaitape was deep at 85 feet, so we only anchored long enough to clear customs, pick up our mail, and do a little exploring around town. Sailors normally try to avoid deep anchorages. The point of anchoring is to keep a boat safe during strong squalls. To do this means putting out at least three to four times the water depth in anchor chain and rode. We carried about 300 feet total, so this anchorage of 85 feet in depth was marginal with our ground tackle. Most people only stayed at that anchorage for a short while.

We didn't need groceries, but took a quick tour of the small town of Vaitape to look for future essentials. We couldn't resist an ice cream stop, the first ice cream we'd had since leaving home.

As we strolled along a path licking our ice cream cones, we came upon a couple with their little boy. We stopped to greet them and introduce ourselves. Our conversation with Scott and Donna went like this:

They: Hi, when did you folks come in?

We: Just arrived. You?
They: Last night.
We: Where are you from?
They: Washington.
We: We are, too. Where?
They: Seattle.
We: Same here! Where in Seattle?
They: North end. You?
We: North end! Our home was 143rd and Ashworth.

They had lived about a half-block from us. We often had seen Donna walk by with Nathaniel in a stroller. Again, small world, and the second couple we'd met from Seattle.

We moved out of Vaitape's deep anchorage and motored close to an uninhabited island, Toopua, and anchored in 35 feet of water. The clear turquoise water allowed us to easily see the bottom. We rowed ashore to a white sandy beach lined with coconut palms. Although no one lived on the island, there was a small copra harvesting operation. Coconuts were collected, split open, the meat pried out and placed on a raised platform shaded by a tarp. Later, it was bagged and shipped off to be squeezed into coconut oil, mostly for cooking and cosmetics.

In addition to coconut palms, there were orange trees and what we learned were vanilla plants.

Bora Bora is as beautiful as postcards describe. The ocean couldn't be bluer, the hills lush and green. Besides the island of Bora Bora, there are several small uninhabited islands within the reef. We were the only ones anchored off Toopua.

We spent a lot of time surface diving in Bora Bora, adding to my shell collection. We devised a good plan to let the shells age without smelling up the boat by putting them in a mesh bag and hanging it under water off the stern. Tiny sea creatures could get in and clean the shells out for us. Then I'd clean them again on shore with oxalic acid. We also found many unoccupied shells in good shape.

Toopua was our home for one week. One day Bruce rowed our dinghy two and a half miles to Vaitape to check for mail and to pick up bread and fresh fruit and vegetables. It was a calm, quiet morning and he thought it would be fun to do. I didn't go with him because I didn't want to add weight to the boat. He had to work hard enough going that distance. At times like this we missed our speedy double kayak, but carrying it onboard would have taken too much deck space.

It was time to move over to Vaitape and take care of business before leaving. As we tried to weigh anchor, Bruce realized our anchor chain was wrapped around coral. He started the engine and tried to jockey the boat back and forth, but it held fast. Bruce went into the water with snorkeling gear and diving weights, and free-dived the 35 feet. It took three or four dives to work the chain free. I was impressed with Bruce's lung capacity to free dive that deep. That's about the depth we used to go with SCUBA gear.

American operated *Hotel Oa Oa* in Vaitape extended an open invitation to boaters to tie up at their dock, which is unusual. We moored on the hotel's floats where several other boats had tied up for the duration of their stay in Bora Bora. Boaters were encouraged to use the hotel's fresh water, their garbage facilities, and their free book-exchange library. They also offered reasonably-priced laundry services. The hotel had one of the town's nicest restaurants and a friendly bar.

Impunity at anchor near Motu Tapu Island

Copra harvesting operation on Toopua Island

Amazingly, we met more people from the Seattle area, Dan a teacher at Rainier Beach High School, and Alice, a chemist. Another couple, more recently from Oregon but who had lived in Seattle, Connie and Vern, were also headed for American Samoa next, as we were.

Although we had loved our little uninhabited island of Toopua, there were no roads and it was quite heavily forested. We longed to get out and really walk, but found the hiking in Viatape frustrating. The village had streets, but they seemed to service only commercial buildings or private housing. We couldn't find a way out of town without going through people's private yards.

One of our business errands was to redeem our bonds, since Bora Bora was our last French Polynesian stop. While having our $1,700 bonds refunded with the bank official, a Frenchman, we asked how we could hike without going through private property. That next weekend, he and a group of kids and a few teachers were going to hike Mount Otemanu and we were welcomed to join them. "Tell your friends," he said. "All are welcome. Bring your lunch and lots of water to drink."

We spread the word among the yachties and several joined us. Our instructions were to meet him in front of the bank at eight the next morning, a Saturday. When we arrived, about thirty 12- to 14-year old kids, all with palm tree saplings in backpacks, four teachers carrying shovels, and our banker had gathered. As we headed out, we crossed in back of what looked like private property. We were impressed that many of the hikers, including the banker, were barefoot.

Almost immediately, the hike went straight up. We followed a path, but much of the time we used vines

Hiking up Mount Otemanu

and small trees to pull ourselves up. At times, our French banker positioned himself at strategic places to help people over particularly rough spots. I admired the stamina of those kids carrying trees.

As the trail wound around the mountain, it often gave us a view of the harbor. Our boat appeared to be a dot in the water from this vantage. The different depths of water as it covered coral reefs dazzled us in shades of blues and greens.

When we stopped to rest, we perched on the steep hill. I didn't find it restful hanging on to something so I didn't slide back down the mountain, or pitch off its steep sides.

The hike up took about three grueling hours. Near the 2,379-foot top, the kids and teachers planted the coconut palm trees. The theory was that a palm tree planted at the top of the mountain would shed coconuts that would roll down the hill to start new coconut trees. Their purpose was to avoid erosion and to replace trees that had died.

We ate our lunches and then the group more or less disbursed. The teachers and banker took the kids back down and we left as we felt like it. I found the trip down far more daunting than going up. To look down those steep hills and descend into a void was far more challenging than clawing my way up.

At one point we could clearly see a trail of people hiking Mount Pahia. With sheer rock to climb to its very top, Mount Pahia, at 2,176 feet, is a rougher hike than Mount Otemanu.

That evening we met several of our new friends at the hotel restaurant. There were a couple of other restaurants in the village, but we felt some obligation to eat at the hotel, since they were so generous to boaters.

Sunday another couple, Kathy and Bill, stopped by our boat and invited us to join them for a walk with the ultimate destination to the ice cream shop. Later, we would also deepen our friendship with these two in American Samoa.

A recent law dictated that boaters could no longer stay in French Polynesia for the hurricane season, as had been our original plan. The exception was if the boater also worked there. We could understand that the local government didn't want to be stuck with the costs of hurricane damage. We needed to keep moving and get to the safety of Pago Pago, American Samoa, to get ourselves secured before bad weather.

Early Monday morning we took a quick trip into town to pick up fresh bread and produce, then loaded the dinghy on board. Since we were tied to a moorage, we didn't have to weigh anchor, but simply cleared customs, untied the boat, and left this Pacific island paradise.

Boats in Vaitape harbor viewed from Mount Otemanu

Even the captain has to take a bath

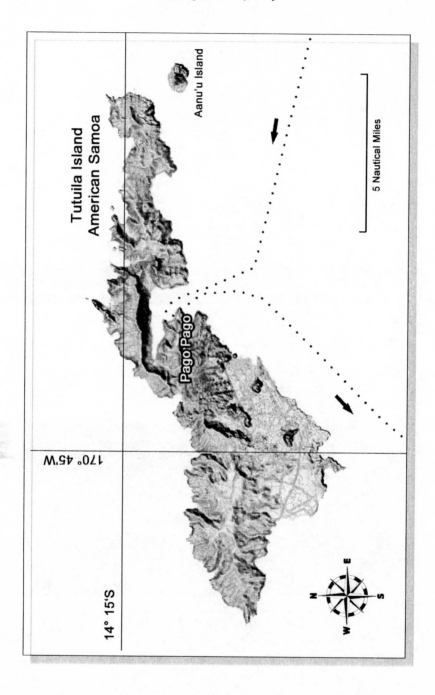

A Safe Harbor – American Samoa

Log Entry—October 11, 1989: We have a little tagalong, a pilotfish.

The hurricane season was fast approaching, and we felt pressure to get to a safe harbor. With moderate winds, we averaged between four and five knots. After a sudden squall, we passed Maupiti Island, leaving it to port under full main and the genoa.

At sea we again followed the Maritime Mobile Net's schedule with our daily check-in and resumed patching phone calls to the family. We listened at least twice a day to weather reports, tracking low pressure areas and hoping we wouldn't have an early hurricane season.

On the first day out of Bora Bora, when checking the jib and looking over the bow, Bruce noticed we had a little tag-along, a pilotfish. Silver with dark vertical stripes, the pilotfish was about 12 inches long. Often seen swimming under the jaws of sharks, pilotfish feed off parasites of their hosts. In our case, it was swimming under the "jaw" of *Impunity*, just to the side of the bow. It kept up with us for four days. We wondered what he ate. Did he find food on our bow?

For awhile, we averaged 125 nautical miles a day; but settled into 100. The smooth passage from Bora Bora to American Samoa was blessedly uneventful. Under these steady conditions, I managed to cook more involved meals. The passage was so consistent, once Bruce adjusted the sails after the initial rain squall, we sailed day-in, day-out with the same configuration, never changing sails or even adjusting the wind-vane steering. It was probably the smoothest sail of the journey.

My night watches, 10:00 to 2:00, were peaceful, allowing me to sit in the stern and soak up the serenity of the calm seas and steady wind, listening as *Impunity* swished through the seas. I continued to set our kitchen timer for every 15 minutes, lest I fall asleep, but I rarely did. This was a dream passage.

In the afternoons, Bruce rigged up a bit of shade with a tarp and we continued with our "sea reading." James Herriot's stories came alive with Bruce's rich voice, especially when he used his great British Highland accent. *All Things Bright and Beautiful* made us long to live in a rural area when we returned home. We'd pretty much had it with city traffic and noise. Getting a dog was also high on our to-do list. We'd read *Diet for a Small Planet* and learned how to manage gardens and stock in a relatively small space. We loved what we were doing right then, but also enjoyed planning for the future.

Pilot fish leading the way to Samoa

The pleasant ten-day passage flew by. Approaching American Samoa in the dark, we gave ourselves plenty of sea-room and slowly sailed back and forth 10 miles offshore until around 3:30, arriving at the harbor entrance just at sunrise.

Pago Pago, pronounced Pong-oh Pong-oh, Harbor is a large natural inlet in the central south coast of Tutuila Island. The harbor is shaped like a boot, accommodating private yachts in the "toe" of the boot.

Looking up, Pago Pago is surrounded by steep hills, covered by lush green tropical growth. But looking at our immediate surroundings, my first reaction to Pago Pago was horror: horror at the filth, at the noise, at the smell. After all the beauty we'd seen, Pago Pago was probably the worst harbor I'd *ever* seen. And to think we were going to be here five months!

The island's diesel electrical generators were right next to the harbor and the roar was deafening. I couldn't imagine ever getting used to that noise. I didn't know what the decibel level was, but it couldn't have been good for our ears. It was hard to carry on a normal conversation on deck.

Both Starkist and Chicken-of-the-Sea tuna processing plants were also located at the harbor, their boats tied up to the company docks, and the smells emitting from the plants were awful. Although these were American plants, most of the boats supplying them were Korean or Taiwanese. The harbor water, a dirty brown, was filthy with plastic bags, garbage, and oil slicks. I even saw a dead pig float by. It was rumored that the processing plants pumped their waste right into the bay. My mood was as bleak as my surroundings.

We arrived on a Saturday, but couldn't clear customs until Monday. We were instructed to find a temporary spot, and then come back Monday to officially check in.

There didn't seem to be any restrictions against our doing a little touring, even though we hadn't cleared customs. I felt desperate to get out of the harbor. Every one of my senses revolted from the surrounding sight, smell and noise. We rowed ashore, rigorously avoiding any splashes from the contaminated water, and walked a short distance into Pago Pago to catch a bus. While we waited for a bus, we passed the time people-watching.

Samoans wear colorful clothes and both men and women wear wrap-around skirts, called lava-lavas. The men wear regular shirts or tank tops; women wear blouses or tee-shirts. Surprisingly, even in skirts, the men look very muscular and masculine. The Police Department was in the same building as the post office and waiting for our bus we noticed the Chief of Police standing outside, wearing a uniform shirt and lava-lava, his badge on a pocket and a holstered gun at his waist. He was not a man you'd take lightly.

The small vibrantly-colored buses were family owned and operated. Music blasted from a loudspeaker. We rocked along in the bus, nodding along to the loud music and watching our cheerful fellow passengers. Before long, we were in lovely surroundings. Lush countryside and nice, though modest, homes abounded. Many of the houses had raised graves in their front yards with ornate markers. In Samoa, family members are most commonly buried at home.

When the roads wound around to ocean beaches, the view was pristine, the beaches spotless and free of litter. What a contrast to Pago Pago Harbor!

In 1872 the high chiefs of the tribes of the eastern Samoan islands gave America permission to establish a naval base in exchange for military protection. After the 1899 Treaty of Berlin, the eastern Samoan Islands became territories of the United States and later became known as American Samoa. Today, though still considered an American territory, American Samoa is self-governed under a constitution that became effective on July 1, 1967.

There are seven islands in American Samoa. The main island, Tutuila, is 20 miles long and up to five miles wide, and is home to the majority of its people. We traveled for several miles without seeing anything except hills and lush growth, then here and there we passed through small villages. That year, the population of American Samoa was 37,000.

My step-sister and her husband had lived in American Samoa for a few years, he as a transportation advisor. They lived in nice housing and had loved Samoa. At my suggestion, Bruce asked the Harbor Master if he knew Dick and MaryLou Berg. It was as though Bruce had mentioned the Harbor Master's long-lost brother. Bruce told him our relationship and suddenly we had a good friend. Interestingly, the Harbor Master, a Samoan, was married to a woman from the States and they had lived in Snohomish, Washington, a small community not far from Seattle. Again, small world.

Because of the hurricane potential, it is required, or at least strongly suggested, that boats be secured to something more solid than normal boat anchors. Through the Harbor Master, Bruce made arrangements to have a commercial diver connect us to a substantial anchor, one already permanently placed in the water. We were assigned our mooring for the hurricane season, November 1 to April 1. We paid $200 for the season, which to us seemed a fair price to be in a safe harbor. Once assigned a season's mooring, boats are expected to stay in place, which meant any sight-seeing would be by foot or by bus.

The commercial diver, a fellow from Vancouver, B.C. hooked us up to a 1,200-pound ship's anchor with heavy-duty chain, but as the day wore on, we could see that with strong winds or tides, we might swing into a neighboring yacht, a 54-foot schooner. Although the people were gracious about it, the situation would be a constant worry. Bruce talked to the Harbor Master who said he'd send the diver back out.

In the meantime, our boats came dangerously close to each other, so the neighboring owners, Bea and Walt, suggested we tie our boat to theirs, the *Galatea*, which we did. Even though we appreciated

Bea and Walt's generous offer, it was far from ideal. Being tied to another boat offered a definite lack of privacy. With the roar of the generator, we couldn't comfortably converse with them on deck.

The Harbor Master said a diver would be at our boat the next morning. No show. Bruce called the diver via VHF radio. He'd said he'd be there by 11:00. No show. Bruce called again and the diver said he'd be over in 15 minutes. No show. Bruce went back to the Harbor Master and told him our problem. The Harbor Master called the diver and the guy immediately came out and adjusted the chain to keep us a safe distance from the schooner. So, finally, we were set.

Our position in the bay was about as good as it would get. It was situated pretty close to shore and was as far away as possible from the noisy generators on land. Arriving a little early had given us the advantage of a more ideal spot. Boats were now arriving in a steady stream, one or two a day. Some were anchored directly in front of the generators. I didn't know how they could stand the noise.

Impunity was about average in size with the other boats in the harbor, which ranged from 30- to 60-feet long. Most had two people aboard, although there were some families, including one family of nine. The children were either home-schooled or they attended school on the island. Most of the kids who also had attended school in the States found they were far ahead of their Samoan classmates.

A few boats were permanently anchored and, of course, they had the ideal spots. Those boaters usually worked in American Samoa, either on a permanent or temporary basis. One boater I talked to said they'd sailed into Samoa and would never sail out. The trip had been a nightmare, she said, and, when they were ready to leave, they'd fly home. In the meantime, her husband worked there as an advisor. Another boater worked in a boat supply store, another was a teacher.

Samoa had a radio station which was nice for music, local, national and international news. They apparently weren't well sponsored because they played the same five commercials throughout every day.

We formed a local VHF radio net with the other yachties and set up an 8:00 a.m. schedule. It was a wonderful way to share news, learn where to purchase things, and make general announcements. Even the old-timers, those who permanently lived in the harbor, joined our radio net.

Clean water was available, but with the frequent rains and our awning, we were able to capture enough to keep our tank and five-gallon jugs full. Many people went ashore daily to fill containers with fresh shore water.

A few years earlier, yachties had built a freshwater shower on shore and housed it in a wooden shed with no roof. What a delight having a freshwater shower in that hot, sultry climate. Toward the end of the day, we rowed ashore and cooled off with a shower. The water wasn't heated, but it always felt wonderful. Sometimes there were a couple people ahead of us, but we enjoyed visiting with our neighbors while we waited our turn.

Vern and Connie, whom we had met in Bora Bora, arrived and we decided to share the cost of a rented car to tour the island. This wasn't something we could do often, but it was such a worthwhile day. We were able to go places a bus didn't go. We drove to beautiful little villages, spoke with friendly people, and saw miles of pristine beach. We found a nice beach to swim and snorkel.

The fale (fah-lay), the traditional Samoan house, is still seen, but many were wiped out in 1964 when hit by a severe cyclone. The government helped replace housing, but would only condone houses made with cement block. Some fales still stand and are used for beach houses, meeting places and ceremonies. A traditional fale is round with a grass-thatched roof held up by wood poles. The floor is either made from coral gravel, or is a raised wooden platform. For privacy or for protection from wind and rain, the sides can be enclosed by lowering shades made from tapa, a cloth made from bark.

We enjoyed Vern and Connie's company and had much in common with them. They had lived in Malaysia for a few years where he was Peace Corps assistant director. We had been in The Gambia, West Africa with the Peace Corps. He was now retired after having served for sixteen years as a substance abuse counselor in Oregon. Connie had taught for several years in special education with children who had reading disabilities. Connie and I had many shared interests, including a background in classical music.

We decided to end our day with dinner at a Chinese restaurant we could see from the harbor. Bruce happened to be driving as the three of us watched for the restaurant. He bypassed it, so turned into a driveway to turn around. Two big Samoan fellows signaled him to stop. One stood in front of the car with his arms crossed, feet wide apart, wearing a lava lava, and the other stood in back of the vehicle taking the same stance.

Bruce got out of the car to explain we only wanted to turn around, but the fellow wouldn't talk to him.

Bruce got back into the car. "I don't know what's going on."

It was hot, so we rolled down the windows. A girl, a teenager, sitting on a porch, said to us, "This is prayer time for the village. We call it `sah.' Wait a few minutes and you can go."

Well, fine. That's all we needed to know. We gladly waited, but resented these fellows and their power trips, not willing to explain their custom to strangers.

On the 8:00 net the next morning, we shared our experience with the others so that they would be warned about village prayer time. One of the yachties who lived aboard and worked ashore said that when he first arrived in Samoa he was jogging through a village during prayer time and was attacked by two men and held to the ground. "You guys got off easy," he said.

Samoans were what I would call fiercely Christian. In any event, we learned not to interfere with prayer time. Each village selects its own prayer time, so you don't really know when that might be.

One day we had gone ashore to pick up our mail at the post office and do a little grocery shopping. We got caught in a rainstorm and returned to the boat drenched to the skin. It rained for hours. Suddenly, the harbor was full of even more plastic bags, plastic bottles and just plain garbage. The Samoans often threw their garbage into gullies and when it rained that hard, the garbage was washed into the harbor. It was awful.

After we'd been in American Samoa a week, a yachtie suggested we have a swap-meet on shore to exchange our unnecessary items. What a great idea. We had all been at sea long enough to know what we needed and what was excess. We had been given two wide-based coffee mugs with non-skid bottoms.

They worked great, but didn't conveniently fit into any of our shelves. They were snapped up immediately. Bruce found an outboard motor for the dinghy at a reasonable price. It would be nice to always not have to row. Besides trading, the event was a great way to meet our neighbors.

As we introduced ourselves, a couple approached us and we chatted for a bit. They were also from Seattle. She asked which boat was ours.

"*Impunity*," I said and pointed it out to her.

"*Impunity. Impunity.* I've seen that boat and wondered why anyone would call their boat *Impunity*. Are you people attorneys? That's more of a legal term, isn't it? I can't imagine calling a boat *Impunity*." Her husband took a step backwards.

I was taken aback. I loved our boat's name, which means freedom from harm or fear. "What's your boat's name?" I asked, wanting to get the topic off our boat before I said something I'd regret.

"Well," she hesitated, "*Hunky Dory*." Her husband grinned. We changed the subject.

Although the noise and harbor filth took some getting used to, all in all we felt American Samoa was a good place to wait out the hurricane season.

Daily Life in Pago Pago

Log Entry—January 27, 1990:   *Weather forecasters report the beginnings of a tropical depresssion developing within the Intertropical Convergence Zone*

*B*ruce and I fell into a nice routine in American Samoa. We're early risers, so would usually eat breakfast before the local 8:00 VHF radio net. First on the net's agenda was any emergency news followed by roll-call, then people came up with questions and announcements. Bruce became the "weather monger" and would give weather reports for the surrounding area. The organized net seemed so "American" as we worked together to make our lives in American Samoa easier.

To talk specifically to another boater, we'd call on the shared frequency, then switch to a side channel. Of course, it wasn't really private—anyone could listen—but we avoided using the channel set aside for group discussions.

Forty-one boats anchored in the harbor, most of whom were transients like us. Boaters usually referred to each other by boat names, such as: "Let's have the *Tainuis* over for dinner." We rarely knew anyone's last name, but often referred to first names and the name of their boat.

One morning a yachtie couple announced they had foul weather gear for sale. Bruce had torn his jacket on our rough passage off the Oregon coast so we were able to replace it. He didn't need it in Samoa, but would on our return trip home.

We began to expand our friendships. My step-sister, MaryLou Berg and her husband Dick had dear friends in Samoa, Marge and Keith Landrigan. Mary Lou had written Marge saying that we would be contacting them.

Motoring ashore in our dinghy, we called the Landrigans, making a date with Marge for lunch at a restaurant near the harbor. It was wonderful having contact with someone who lived there. Marge asked if I played bridge, and learning I did, invited me to be a substitute in her group. Another yachtie woman who had lived with her husband aboard for several years, played regularly and had a car, so I would ride with her.

I had the great pleasure of playing bridge the following Wednesday. There were two tables, eight ladies, and it was fun hearing the "inside scoop" of living in American Samoa. Some were born in Samoa, some the States, and one player was from New Zealand. During our five months there I substituted a dozen or so times.

I found I needed to expand my wardrobe. The Samoans didn't have much leg showing, so I needed knee-length shorts. It was hard to believe, but it was too hot for tank-tops in that climate. Luckily, loose-fitting blouses were comfortable, inexpensive and readily available.

Thanksgiving was around the corner, and the yachties made arrangements to have our celebration at the Yacht Club, which would otherwise be closed for the holiday. The Yacht Club wasn't a fancy building; in fact, it was left over from World War II when it had been used for officers' quarters. But it was spacious, breezy and made a great place to gather.

Many of the boaters in the harbor spent a great deal of time at the Yacht Club, but we normally went only on Friday nights when they served a choice of hamburgers or fishburgers. It was fun talking to the other yachties and also to other boaters who were permanent residents of American Samoa, mostly people originally from the States.

Since we had found so much to do, our immediate surroundings became more tolerable. We grew accustomed to the loud generators and learned to be careful to avoid the disgusting harbor water. Having personal contacts made a huge difference in our lives. We were making good friends and that went a long way toward contentment.

Vern and Connie invited us to join them for another bus excursion. We rocked along to loud Samoan music in the mini-bus. We neared a beach, climbed off the bus and wandered around until we came upon "Tisa's Beach." We met Tisa, a lovely Samoan, who served us beer at her little outdoor bar. She invited us to swim on her beach, and offered the use of her shower room to change our clothes. The unique shower had three walls and an open-air side with a sweeping view of the sea.

Swimming at Tisa's Beach with its strong current was a bit dicey. Connie and I stayed close to shore, but Bruce and Vern went farther out. They later told us they had to really fight the current to get back. Snorkeling wasn't as good as in other parts of the South Pacific. The colorful fish and coral weren't as plentiful, but it felt good to swim in the clear open sea.

After showering, we climbed back on a bus and explored the small village of Tula where many Samoans live with extended family. Some communities were more welcoming than others. Several beaches were private, or rather we'd have to go through private property to get to them, so we considered them off-limits.

Although exploring was fun, we also relished hanging out at home on our boat. Bruce maintained the engine, changed oil, sanded and revarnished brightwork, and attended to other repairs. We no longer had to run the engine to keep the batteries charged as the solar panels worked sufficiently for our electrical needs. Again, we were thankful not to have refrigeration. Those who did had to run their engine even at anchor in order to keep their refrigerators operating. It not only took fuel, but running the engines made their boats much hotter.

I managed the house-keeping, cooking, and laundry. We both wrote letters and enjoyed reading each other's letters home. And, of course, we read a lot of books, regularly trading reading material with other boaters.

Bruce noticed a growth of long-necked barnacles and other marine critters on the bottom of our dinghy. He had painted anti-fouling hull paint on *Impunity* just before we left, but not the dinghy. He took the little boat ashore and cleaned its bottom.

Although there was a laundry nearby, with fresh water in plentiful supply, I still washed most of our clothes and the galley towels by hand and hung them out to dry. If it rained, they got an extra rinse. Every couple of weeks I washed sheets and bath towels at the laundry which was within walking distance of the harbor.

When waiting for my laundry, I often saw a fellow there who seemed to be quite popular among the local people. By his actions and mannerisms I realized he was probably a fa'afafine, a role widely accepted among the Samoan people. Fa'afafine' translates "in the manner of a woman." To be a fa'afafine one has to be "Samoan, born a man, but feel like a woman." Traditionally, fa'afafine follows the training of women's daily work. They are usually the caretakers of their elderly parents since brothers and sisters are married with families of their own. Although fa'afafine may have sexual relations with other men or with women, they rarely form sexual relationships with other fa'afafines. Samoans do not label fa'afafine as being "gay" or "homosexual," but rather consider them as a third gender, a gender well accepted in the Samoan culture. Interestingly, there appeared to be no equivalent for a woman.

Another boat arrived weeks after we did. We had met Kathy and Bill in Bora Bora and it had taken them all that time to get to Samoa due to incredibly bad luck. They had blown out two sails, had engine trouble and gone aground in the Cook Islands. Whether bad judgment, faulty planning, or bad luck, we were always amazed at some cruisers' lack of pre-paredness.

Samoan air temperatures ranged from 85- to 90-degrees with high humidity. I can't imagine life there without our awning, though many boats in the harbor didn't have them. Besides the shade, the awning allowed us to collect rain water nearly every day, which kept our water tank and jugs full of fresh, pure rain water. When it rained, it poured. Sometimes we'd get as much rain in one hour as Seattle would in a month. But after a rain, it would clear up and turn hot and sunny.

Using a tarp, Bruce rigged a wind funnel for the forward hatch, right above our bed. With the funnel over the open hatch we still had the benefit of fresh air breezes, but avoided the rain.

Even with all the rain, plentiful sunshine kept our batteries charged by solar panels. We were glad we had solar rather than a wind generator. For one thing, finding a safe place for a wind generator and its sharp blades is often a challenge. Then, too, if the wind is too strong, a wind generator has to be shut down or it can self-destruct.

After a hard rain, Bruce usually climbed into the dinghy and bailed out four to six inches of rain water. One very wet evening, after watching a movie on VCR with Vern and Connie aboard *Tainui*, we had to bail our dinghy before we could return to *Impunity*. As we made our way home, we stopped at several boats that had hard dinghies—inflatables would not sink—and suggested to them they bail their dinghies. Most were so full they would have sunk by morning.

About once a week, someone announced on the VHF radio that a local woman was on the dock with fresh, home-made bean burritos for sale. We often bought two or three from her and then reheated them for dinner, usually topping them with grated cheese. It was a treat not having to cook.

Someone on the net announced that a Tongan woman had offered to teach yachties traditional Tongan weaving and that the classes would be held in a nearby building. Several of us decided to go and I was so glad I did. Fanny, the teacher, furnished our first materials and told us where we could get more on our own. I had never woven before, but found I really loved it. Tongan weaving involves using palm veins as the bundle and strips of dried pandanus leaves for the wrap.

We students made a boat-shape tray for our first effort. After that we were on our own but with the benefit of Fanny's guidance. At the public market, I bought a bundle of palm veins, which Samoans use for brooms. They're about three feet long. Pandanus leaves are sometimes available at the market, but I couldn't find any the day I looked, so asked a vendor about them. She said she'd bring a supply for me the next day. They come rolled in an18-inch circle. The wide leaves then had to be cut into narrow strips to wrap around the bundle. I happily sat under our awning and wove to my heart's content, making trays and eventually bowls. I loved the creativity of weaving and seeing something take shape from my own handiwork.

Sometimes several of the yachties met at a waterfront park for a meal. One afternoon I made a potato salad for a potluck birthday celebration dinner. It's amazing how much food is generated at a potluck.

It was always fun to learn more about the sailors. Most of them planned to take five years or more for their trips. Ours was the shortest trip of anyone there.

Mary learned Tongan-style basket weaving

Most of them were retired, or were working along the way. Up to that time, we were comparable to the others in distance traveled so far, about 7,000 miles.

A locally famous hotel, Rainmaker, occasionally had interesting programs. One evening we attended a show that featured four Polynesian dancing styles: Hawaiian, Tahitian, Marquesan, and Samoan. Samoan dancing was the most aggressive, particularly the fire knife dancers. At one time, the hotel had been managed by Pan American World Airways but now was run by Samoans. We found it quite run-down and learned several of the guest rooms were unusable. The meals, however, were good. After dinner I went into the bathroom which was carpeted, but wet. Water squished over the top of my sandals. Eeew!

Thanksgiving at the Yacht Club was a huge success. The group pitched in and bought two turkeys and two couples volunteered to roast them, one at the club, the other at their friend's house nearby. Together with Vern and Connie, we made the stuffing and I volunteered to make gravy. Otherwise, it was pot-luck. Thirty adults and six children attended. What fun! We loved celebrating our traditional patriotic and family holiday with fellow Americans. Getting together with other expatriates helped stave off homesickness. Our families at home were very much on our minds.

Our thoughts turned to Christmas. At the little shopping center near the harbor, a small variety store carried tee-shirts. We bought a Samoan-theme shirt for every member of the family—kids and grandkids—ten in all.

Our friends Vern and Connie planned to go home to Oregon for two months during the Christmas season. Even though they were circumnavigating, it was their plan always to return home for Christmas.

We took one last excursion with them before they left. Catching a family-owned bus, we visited a shop someone had told us about that sold hand-made crafts. We bought a lovely little wooden bowl for Bruce's parents for Christmas. We climbed on another bus and visited Pago Pago International Airport, where we had lunch. The National Oceanic and Atmospheric Administration (NOAA) has a weather station at the airport and we watched as they launched a weather balloon.

We said our goodbyes to Vern and Connie. Two months was a long time to be gone. I didn't envy them the trip, but it was important to them.

Jack and Donna from *Zingara* were celebrating their wedding anniversary and they invited us to join them for dinner. Jack had retired from the Santa Barbara school district in California and Donna was a nurse. We liked being with them and over time enjoyed many meals aboard each others' boats.

Bruce caught the flu bug that had been going around. Other than mild seasickness, it was the first time on this trip either of us had been ill, and he was hit hard with six days of a rising temperature, as high as 102 degrees. Poor, miserable fellow. In that heat and humidity, having a fever was tough. Luckily, I didn't catch it.

As Christmas approached, the Samoans definitely got into the spirit with decorated stores and Christmas music on the radio. Samoans don't hesitate being blatantly Christian, and separation of church and state wasn't practiced at that time. Local business people, government employees and bankers were expected to take time off from work to rehearse for these Christmas programs. For two weeks before Christmas, wonderful outdoor concerts were held every night at a large park, with various church, school and business company choirs. We attended a program one night and were so impressed. Four different groups sang traditional Christmas carols and other pieces we didn't recognize. Between choral performances scripture was read, mostly the Christmas story from the four gospels. And the drumming! We could have listened to the drumming all night. The concert ended with Handel's "Hallelujah Chorus" from the "Messiah." The music resonated with me for hours afterward.

A week before Christmas we extended an invitation to everyone on boats in the harbor to join us on *Impunity* for Christmas Eve day, from 1:00 to 4:00. I announced the invitation during the morning net. Typical of our group and our careful schedule planning, one of the gals responded, "That's going to be a busy day. Why don't we make it a couple days before that?"

I laughed. "This isn't really a discussion, Donna, it's an invitation." She laughed, too. "Oh, right. I get so used to discussing everything."

Bruce and I got the boat ship-shape, I baked cookies, and we lined up plenty of snacks. Interestingly, it was the first time we had bought ice since we'd been in the South Pacific. Although some people bought ice daily, we were used to drinking beverages either hot or "room" temperature. But we bought plenty of beer and soda and had bottles and cans chilling in a tub of ice.

Throughout the afternoon people rowed or motored in their dinghies and tied up to *Impunity*. It was amazing having that many people aboard. Our boat sank almost to its scuppers with the extra load. It was a wonderful party and really inspired the Christmas spirit.

Like Thanksgiving, our group had the Yacht Club to ourselves for Christmas Day. We chipped in for a couple of hams, and otherwise brought pot luck. After dinner we played a gift exchange game where the first person opens a wrapped gift. The next person can either take a gift that's been opened or choose a wrapped gift. Most of the yachties attended and even invited shore friends. Our Christmas away from home was delightful though we felt occasional twinges of homesickness. We both missed our families.

Postal service was blessedly regular and it was a short distance to walk to mail or pick up letters. The post office looked much like those in the States, except chickens ran around the parking lot. The cost of postage was also the same as the States, since it is an American Territory. We received a stream of Christmas cards and they became part of our boat's Christmas decorations.

Through a bridge contact, we were invited to a private home to watch the Rose Bowl game on New Year's Day. Two other couples from the harbor were also invited, one of them the lady with whom I rode to bridge. We're not enthusiastic TV sports watchers, but it was fun visiting with the other guests and spending time in their private back yard. The hosts served a lovely brunch. Bruce and I loaded our plates, slid open the screen door, carefully closing it behind us, and went out to the patio to sit at a picnic table. One of the other yachtie couples joined us.

The third harbor couple was still loading their plates inside. I didn't know them well, but I knew he was a cartoonist and many of the boaters in the harbor had hired him to draw their boat in that ex- aggerated way political cartoonists do. The woman came out first, sliding the screen door shut behind her. Her husband followed, but to our amazement, he simply walked through the screen, knocking out the entire frame and screen and stepping on it, never acting as though anything strange had just happened, only stepping a little higher than he otherwise might have. I think he may have had a few too many.

The man's wife scowled at him and said, "How could you do that?" Her husband looked puzzled and shrugged.

One of the other fellows said, "I know! You're a cartoonist, and that kind of thing happens all the time in cartoons." The cartoonist shrugged again. It was actually rather strange.

About once a week we planned a hike, either on the surrounding hills or elsewhere on the island, often sharing our experiences on the net. Soon people were asking if they could join us. One yachtie whose husband worked ashore said to us, "You folks *do* things. I can't stand sitting at the yacht club all the time like so many of these people do."

Our hikes usually were early morning affairs; it was too hot in the afternoons for that kind of exertion. One day, six of us hiked seven miles on a ridge across the bay from the harbor. We had packed our lunch and munched at the crest overlooking the sea.

On the radio, we heard about an agriculture fair being held at the American Samoa Community College, their seventh annual. Bruce and I took a bus to the event. People there seemed pleased that we'd come. We viewed displays of land erosion and its effect on the island. We read fishing industry information, and admired displays of fruits, vegetables and even livestock. Lunch was $3 a plate, a chicken/vegetable noodle dish and a pineapple custard turnover.

Marge Landrigan, my bridge contact and friend of my step-sister, invited us to their home for the weekend. It would be our first night spent ashore since this journey began. Their home was on family land, their portion being six of 33 acres. Marge was half-Samoan, and although she and Keith met and married in California, they had lived in Samoa for twenty years. Their large and airy home was filled with interesting South Pacific relics, carvings, woven trays and bowls, and exquisitely designed tapa cloth wall hangings. Two other couples were invited for dinner, making a party of eight. We feasted on barbecued fish, a chicken dish, rice, veggies and a great cake for dessert. Sleeping in the king-size bed on solid ground was a treat though it felt odd after so many nights being rocked to sleep.

The next day Marge took us to visit her 85 year-old mother, Mary Pritchard, a well-known Samoan artist. Her artistic specialty was tapa-cloth and her house was filled with it. The house, a true fale, was open air with a grass-thatched roof and ceiling to floor tapa cloths.

When Keith and Marge dropped us off at the harbor Sunday night, we felt sated and cared for, grateful for good friends who would share their island life with us.

George and Ellen invited us for dessert aboard their boat *Winddancer.* George, a doctor, had signed a one-year contract with the local hospital, as did Ellen, a hearing specialist. They planned to work their way around the world. George had built their 40-foot boat over an eight-year period.

Occasionally people asked Bruce's advice on some boat malfunction. When asked, he went aboard their boats and made suggestions. In a couple of instances, he repaired electronic equipment. He would not take payment, but we did accept a few dinner invitations at local restaurants.

One early morning, I awoke to Bruce, agitated and trying to say something that just didn't make sense. I figured he'd had a bad dream. "It's all right, Bruce, you've had a dream."

"No! Someone's on board!"

He jumped out of bed, stark naked, and ran up on deck. I followed along right behind. Sure enough, a young Samoan, maybe in his late teens, was on our deck. He took one look at Bruce and dove overboard, quickly untying his canoe from our boarding ladder and swimming away, pushing his boat ahead of him as he went. He'd made a pile of items he'd planned to take—pliers, a rope splicing tool, two wrenches, and a knife. Apparently, he'd reached down to the navigation station from the open aft hatch and gathered what he could.

Later Bruce told me he awoke to an unfamiliar noise, a soft little creak. Lying on his back, when he opened his eyes, he saw a dark facing looking down at him through the forward hatch above our bed.

At daylight Bruce went ashore and reported the illegal boarding to the police, but they seemed unconcerned. On that morning's net, Bruce warned the other boaters about it so they could take precautions.

One day Bruce and I took a bus as close as it would get to the Advanced Global Atmospheric Gases Experiment (AGAGE) situated on the northeastern tip of the island, on a ridge overlooking the South Pacific ocean. We hiked in the last mile or so, past the "No vehicles beyond this point" sign. The area has several concrete buildings, but they didn't look as though they were geared for guests. The observatory was established in 1974 with the purpose of testing the air for purity. Because of the trade wind patterns, the air that reaches here at Cape Matatula has traveled across the ocean thousands of uninterrupted miles and is pristine. It seemed odd to me that on the same island the purist air was found and also some of the worst that we'd encountered, in Pago Pago Harbor.

Bruce rarely missed listening to two or three daily weather reports. On January 27, he reported to the morning net the beginnings of a tropical depression developing within the Intertropical Convergence Zone over the Tuvaluan Islands. No one seemed alarmed; no one on shore even talked about it.

The weather began to get nasty, with wind and rain. When we had business on shore, we dashed out between squalls. Harbor waters were rough with choppy waves. We cringed when dirty harbor water splashed on us as we rowed the dinghy to shore.

We wondered how safe this "safe harbor" was.

10

Cyclone *Ofa* Clobbers Samoa

Log Entry—January 30, 1990: Cyclone Ofa is heading right toward us. Time to batten down.

There's really no difference between a hurricane, cyclone, or typhoon. They are all the same weather phenomenon, but the storms are called different names in different places. In the Atlantic and Northeast Pacific, the term "hurricane" is used. The same type of disturbance in the Northwest Pacific is called a "typhoon," and "cyclones" occur in the South Pacific and Indian Ocean.

Whatever we called it, it was time to get serious about protecting our boat, our home. Cyclone Ofa was coming, ready or not. From the prediction, this storm was one of the largest in a decade.

We boaters scurried around, removing anything that would catch the wind. We took down the tarps that Bruce had put around the hatches to keep out rain but let in breeze. The awning had to come down. We took the sails off the booms. Even though they were tied down, they created "windage," sailor-speak for something the wind could catch on. The solar panels and mizzen boom were stowed below decks. We lowered the main boom and tied it securely to the rail. The decks were cleared of cushions and anything that wasn't attached. Bruce took the motor off the dinghy. Everything went below decks. Bruce double-tied everything he could, the lines to the anchors, the dinghy. We checked every system on the boat to make sure it was in working order. The cabin was crammed with all that had been on deck, which troubled my innate sense of order, but I simply had to put up with the clutter.

Every boat in the harbor frantically prepared for the big storm. Bruce took time out to listen to weather reports and shared the storm's progress over the VHF net.

We dashed ashore to get a few supplies, again getting drenched with the filthy harbor water. The nasty weather howled with furious wind and drenching rain, but when we entered the grocery store, all seemed calm. We mentioned something about the cyclone to the clerk and he gave us a blank stare. He knew nothing about it. We asked around, but no one was concerned.

"This is our rainy season," they said.

The local folks kept telling us that nothing had been reported on the radio about a coming cyclone. As we talked, they became more concerned, but still we could tell they didn't feel alarmed since our warning was not "official."

Come to find out, the Pago Pago International Airport had been closed because of high winds. With no planes coming in or out, the weather station was shut down and the forecasters had gone home, leaving the local people without radio weather reports.

When we returned to our boat, we called on the net and suggested that anyone who knew people on shore should warn them. That was easier said than done since cell phones weren't in use yet. Any phoning was done from telephone booths, from offices, or homes. It was scary, knowing that many people didn't have appropriate warning.

A family in the harbor with a child was going to weather the storm ashore at a friend's home and offered to take children from other boats with them. Most of us felt compelled to stay with our boats, do what we could to protect them. It was a nice offer and I'm sure people with children were relieved.

On Friday, February 2, bad weather arrived in earnest. Rain and high winds blew from the northwest, moving southeast toward us. Winds picked up to about 40 knots, gusting in the harbor to 55 knots (about 60 miles per hour). Our barometer fell like a rock.

Nobody in the harbor slept. We left our VHF radios on Channel 16 so that we could hear from each other what was going on.

As a safety precaution, a 30-foot sloop rafted to a 60-foot schooner because the smaller boat wasn't permanently tied to a large harbor anchor. Shortly after midnight Friday, with winds gusting 80 miles per hour, the schooner started dragging their 750-pound anchor across the bay, taking the smaller boat with her. As they slowly pulled the huge anchor, Ed, the skipper of the 30-foot sloop tied to the bigger boat, called another boat they were dragging toward. "Buddy, we're coming down on you."

The response: "We see you, Ed, we're ready." We could hardly believe the calmness in their voices.

Then, for about 45 minutes, we watched in admiration as they tried to run lines among all three boats, all while the boats were swinging and rolling violently. It was an amazing feat of seamanship. Once they finally got the three secured together, they spent the rest of the night with engines running to relieve the tension on the third boat's anchor.

The next morning, Saturday, February 3, the wind eased a bit and Bruce helped the smaller boat move to a sturdy harbor dock. It seemed the storm was calming, but according to weather reports, there was more to come.

Later Saturday the barometer bottomed out and the wind shifted as the cyclone howled down on us. By that evening we felt as though the stuffing had been slapped out of us.

Someone on the net said, "Hey, listen. No generator noise." It had been knocked out, which must have been a concern to people in houses, but to us it was a little less noise, though with the screaming wind it was hard to appreciate.

Strangely, leaves began falling on the deck.

Either Bruce or I was in the cockpit at all times, watching for hazards. Korean and Taiwanese longliners were moored across the bay from us at the tuna processing plants and we didn't have much confidence they had been securely tied. It's possible to fend off other boats or objects in the water, but you have to be alert to catch them before they do any damage.

We wore foul-weather gear, not for warmth but to protect our skin from the stinging, driving rain. To see anything we had to squint against the wind and rain. It was a sinking feeling to watch a wall of wind and water slam into the boat upwind of us and see it almost lay over, their mast seemingly inches from the sea, knowing that we'd be next. Then we'd take the hit, feel a strong jolt, and swing and roll with alarming force. It would pass on, and we'd brace ourselves for the next one.

I saw and heard the corrugated tin roof of a building near the harbor dock rip off and watched as it wobbled through the air toward our boat. I ducked, but it veered off and dropped into the water. That roof could damage a boat, but it was out of reach, and all we could do was report it on the net.

Another night passed with no more than a couple hours sleep.

Sunday we were still at it. The screaming wind and driving rain seemed endless. Fatigue impaired our strength and thinking. There was no way to cook, but we ate crackers and cheese for nourishment.

Sunday evening, probably the worst night, our friends Jack and Donna's boat *Zingara* began dragging their 1,200-pound harbor anchor across the bay. They started their engine to ease the load on the anchor, and then their steering gear broke! Donna quickly packed their backpacks and they were ready to jump ship if their boat hit the rocks. Just in time, they passed over a shallower spot and the anchor dug in again.

On VHF we heard from the family who had gone ashore with all the children. While the woman pre-pared dinner for the crowd, the power went out and the roof of the house blew off. They all crowded into the landlord's house, but then his roof blew off. All they could do was hunker down and wait it out.

Boats are meant to move, to swing and roll. We were probably the safest right where we were, in the harbor, securely anchored. As the wind eased, we could see that *Impunity* suffered no damage—she rode it like a trooper. Our dinghy sank, but when Bruce pulled it up it had only lost the little bow seat, a minor inconvenience.

By Monday things were calm enough that we could venture out. We knew even before going ashore that there would be heavy destruction. Many houses in Samoa aren't solidly built. They don't need to have heavy walls because it never gets really cold. But we weren't prepared for the damage we saw. From our boat, we could see what had been a steep lush mountainside was now ugly jagged tree stumps, revealing houses half blown away, missing roofs and walls, trees and power poles scattered everywhere. We hadn't even known houses were on that hill. Now it was an ugly scarred hillside.

Bruce and I walked through neighborhoods, impressed as people industriously cleared debris, helping one another, and thanking God that no one on that island had been killed. Forty to sixty percent of the homes were either damaged or destroyed in American Samoa. In Western Samoa, 75 miles to the west, seven people were killed and many others injured. Several boats sank in Western Samoa's Apia Harbor. In both American Samoa and Western Samoa, soft fruit crops were destroyed for that year's harvest, primarily bananas, breadfruit and taro.

The main streets were cleared fairly quickly and Bruce and I took a bus out to the airport to see the damage there. The terminal had several broken windows, but the building appeared to be structurally sound. We stopped by the General Services Administration (GSA) to pick up a new American flag. Our flag, new when we left, looked like it had been in a war zone, with frayed seams and edges. GSA had a plentiful supply of good-quality flags of all sizes.

Phone service and electricity were out for some time after the cyclone, but the Samoans were pretty casual about that inconvenience. Many homes were being completely rebuilt, and thousands of corrugated roofs replaced.

The American Red Cross came and we often saw workers out in the field doing what they could to meet the island's emergency needs.

Vern and Connie returned to Samoa after their Christmas holiday, anxious about their boat and how it had ridden out the storm. They found everything intact, but all the bulkheads, overheads and cabin decks were covered with fuzzy green mold. They had closed everything up tight and with the humidity, mold grew with abandon.

A couple of weeks later, a NOAA ship made a routine call to American Samoa. Our friends Keith and Marge Landrigan encouraged us to contact a friend of theirs who worked aboard. Janet, 44, had been with NOAA for several years and worked as an oiler in the engine room. The delightful lady showed us around the ship. They spent about ten months of the year at sea, usually spending four days in each port. When she wasn't at sea with NOAA, she lived aboard her yacht, currently in Texas. We invited Janet to dinner aboard *Impunity*. She was a fun, adventurous lady.

Ralph and Ann, people we met at the Landrigan's when we spent the weekend, invited us to their home for a barbecue and showed an interest in seeing *Impunity*. We had set a date for them to have dinner with us and they were impressed with my cheese souffle, surprised we could produce a meal like that aboard a sailboat. Ralph worked for the State Department in American Samoa and had an aspiration of single-handing to Australia in a dinky little sailboat. We tried to slip in a few ideas during the evening in the hope he might reconsider. In the first place, he didn't know a thing about celestial navigation or even much about electronic navigation equipment. Bruce gave him some literature to read. I suggested he read Robin Grahams' *Dove*, which is a good account of the adventures and also the risks and loneliness of single-handing.

We met several people who had single-handed. It's not an easy thing to do and I personally could not understand why anyone would do it. Our friend Jack had circumnavigated single-handed, but he was a top-rate sailor. Ralph had a lot of enthusiasm, but not much experience. We told him of all our preparations and I think he found it daunting. I could see his wife, Ann, silently cheering us on, subtly, or maybe not so subtly, trying to discourage him. I've wondered since if Ralph made that voyage.

On our "down time," often after dinner, we continued reading aloud to each other. We read two of Robert Fulghum's books, *All I Really Need to Know I Learned in Kindergarten* and *It Was On Fire When I Lay Down on It*. These quiet times, reading aloud, were our favorite times of the day. We didn't miss TV, and other than for a few moments in the morning to hear the news, rarely listened to the radio.

We took a day trip with Vern and Connie to a small island, Auna'u, catching a bus, then a small ferry to the island. Auna'u offered a pristine beach with bountiful shells for our collection, and even a picnic table to enjoy the lunch we'd packed. Cyclone

Ofa had done some damage to this small island, mostly to crops. We found the people more traditional than those in Pago Pago, but friendly and open to our exploring their island. We watched men and boys hunt fruit bats. They made stew of the bats. I felt I'd never be able to get past the smell, sort of like skunk, albeit milder.

Back aboard *Impunity*, I spent every spare moment weaving and by this time had started making gifts for family members. I had found a source for pandanus leaves and palm veins, so I didn't have to worry about running out of materials.

The Samoan government considered doubling the harbor fees, and word was out that the increase would be retroactive to those of us who had been there during the hurricane season. Boaters who worked in Pago Pago and who were "in the know" told us about a government committee meeting being held on that topic. Several of the yachties from the harbor attended the meeting. We appointed a spokesman and he did a good job of summarizing the group's feeling about raising the rates after the fact. Each boat had already paid $200 for the season and the proposal would cost us another $200. When they asked for additional comments, one of the yachties stood and said she was a freelance writer for several sailing magazines and that if this rate went into effect retroactively, she would feel compelled to mention this unfairness in her articles. The government committee said they would take our comments into consideration and let us know their decision. Later we learned they would not impose the new rates on us, but would for future boats coming into the harbor for hurricane seasons.

George and Ellen of *Winddancer* had invited us to join them for a three-day getaway to Ofu, a small neighboring island with a resort. We called to see if the resort was still open for business, thinking they might have suffered from Cyclone Ofa. Somehow, they were spared significant damage, and encouraged us to come ahead. There were still vacancies at the resort, so Vern and Connie were also able to join us.

We caught a small plane at the airport and a 20-minute flight later landed a few yards from the front door of our cabin. The resort was run by a palongi (white person) woman who had met and married a Samoan while he served with the Navy in Norfolk. They were married twelve years before she ever saw Samoa. The resort was from his family property and consisted of their home, a lodge with a kitchen and dining room, five duplex cabins, each with queen size bed and a bathroom with a shower. All meals were in the lodge.

The owner offered us his truck to drive around to see the island. Bruce drove with Vern riding as "shotgun" and I sat in the bed of the truck with the others. It took less than an hour to thoroughly traverse the island. What fun! Ofu was a wonderful getaway for us. The whole three-day weekend with meals cost the two of us $250, including the flight.

The hurricane season appeared to be over and we were ready to move on. It appeared that Bruce and I were going to be the first to depart Samoa. The boat was ready and we'd provisioned with extra food items. We still had plenty of staples, but stocked up on peanut butter, a large tin of pilot crackers, and coffee.

Fanny, my weaving teacher, suggested that the group have a farewell party for me. It was embarrassing since all, or most of us, would soon be leaving. But the group wanted to do it and make it a family

171

pot-luck picnic. Sixteen of us celebrated our last days in Samoa together. I was very touched when Fanny gave me a tapa cloth she had made. To create a tapa involves much labor. The cloth itself, about 24 inches square, was mulberry bark pounded to paper thinness. The particular design of my tapa was flowers, and the dyes used were from roots. Fanny gave me the name of a woman she hoped I'd call on when we reached Tonga, a fellow weaver. I think Fanny felt especially close to me because I was so enthusiastic about weaving.

We were anxious to get underway, but high winds delayed our departure for a week. We had planned to visit Western Samoa, but Apia Harbor was closed to boat traffic because they still hadn't cleared the sunken boats after Cyclone Ofa.

The weather cleared and we hired a professional diver to disconnect us from the harbor anchor. We were finally underway after five months in American Samoa. We set a schedule for 8:30 each morning to call those still in Pago Pago on the net on SSB radio. Many were interested in this leg of our journey since they would soon be following.

It felt good to be away from the generator noise and to be back into clean water. The seas seemed rough, but after all, we'd been tied to an anchor for five months.

We were on our way to the Kingdom of Tonga!

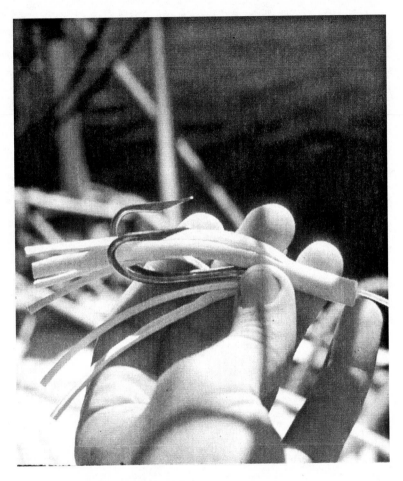

Heavy-duty tackle led to more fishing success

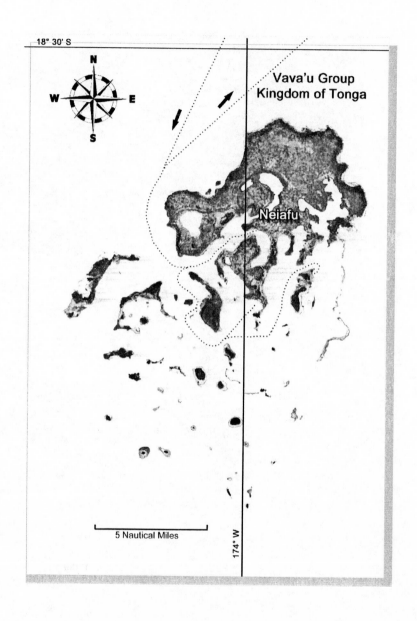

Paradise in The Kingdom of Tonga

Log entry—April 14, 1990: Neiafu, Kingdom of Tonga, looks like what we imagined a frontier town looked like 150 years ago.

O n-the-nose winds made this leg of the journey tough. After a five-month absence from sailing, my stomach rebelled. I wasn't over-the-side sick, but for the first day and a half I didn't feel my best

On the second night, Bruce had gone off watch at 10:00 and just settled down in the midship bunk. I scanned the horizon and went below decks to make a cup of tea. Bruce had put the teakettle on the stove to heat the water for me, so I didn't harness myself into the galley for the quick trip to get my cup and a tea bag. The boat surged up, then suddenly dropped off the back of a wave and threw me backwards across the boat. I landed at the edge of the chart table, hitting my lower back, three inches from my spine on my right side.

I knew immediately that I was hurt, that I'd probably broken a rib. Bruce leapt out of the bunk with my scream as I crashed into the chart table. He wanted me to lie down right away, but I was anxious to see how badly I was hurt, so I insisted on standing my watch, with the understanding I'd call him if I needed to. Reluctantly, he agreed.

Following our normal night watch routine, I set our kitchen timer for every 15 minutes and at that time did a 360-degree horizon check. I also checked the knot-meter, compass, and trim of the sails, to make sure everything was okay. Because the seas were so rough, I sat tucked up under the dodger. By the sixteenth time I stood up on the rocking boat, I knew that nothing vital was broken. But I also knew that I was really hurting and that once I lay down, I'd probably not get up again until we arrived in Tonga.

At the end of my watch Bruce got me settled onto the bunk and that was it for me for the next day and a half, other than brief trips to the head. Keeping our regular ham net schedule, Bruce called Pago Pago and talked to our doctor friend George on *Wind-dancer*. I had already taken aspirin—lots of it. We had stronger pain medication on board, but I was hesitant to take it and be totally "out of it." I knew if I had to I could get up and help Bruce. While George and Bruce talked, another person in Tonga chimed in, introduced himself and said he was a doctor, a fellow yachtie, and was in Neiafu Harbor, Tonga. He'd meet our boat there.

As we approached Tonga, the seas calmed allowing me to gingerly walk around, even prepare meals. Bruce was weary, having run the boat by himself and taken care of me.

We'd carried a boat part from Samoa for another boater and he met us a couple of hours away from Neiafu in his dinghy. He thanked us profusely; he couldn't run his boat without replacing that part. He inquired about my injury. Word spreads quickly, especially with radio conversations and the small sailing community.

We pulled into Neiafu Harbor mid-day and a customs man came aboard first, inquiring about me. He'd heard about my injury on the radio. I was again lying on the bunk, not able to stand comfortably while the boat jostled into place at the wharf for the customs inspection. Then the doctor, the yachtie, came aboard and verified it was likely a broken rib, or a badly bruised one. In any event, the treatment was the same. He gave me ibuprofen, a pain medication I'd never used before, which was more effective than aspirin for me. He offered to tape my torso, but I declined. It was just too hot. He suggested that I could swim, very gently, but no diving off the boat.

As we headed out to find a place to anchor, Bruce put out a fishing line. When in Samoa, he had inquired about fishing gear for tropical waters. The salmon gear we had brought was too light. Now, equipped with 1/8-inch diameter monofilament, 200-pound test line and two-inch hooks, we were in business. From orange plastic tubing we had on hand, Bruce fashioned a lure that resembled a squid. Within minutes we had a nice fish on the line, a small tuna.

Approaching one of the many islands in Vava'u Tonga

Mary rowing ashore to meet neighbors

It felt so good not to be crashing around at sea. Once we were anchored, I carefully climbed down our boarding ladder to enjoy a cooling swim. Now this was the life—a just-caught dinner waiting to be cooked, and me swimming in pristine, clear water. Tonga was blissfully quiet and unbelievably beautiful.

Tonga is an archipelago of one hundred fifty islands, thirty-six of which are inhabited. Four major groups of islands form the Kingdom: the Tongatapu, Ha'apai, Vava'u, and Niua groups. We were anchored near Neiafu, which is part of Vava'u. Tongatapu is the main island and the location of its capital, Nuku'alofa.

The only Pacific Island nation never colonized by a foreign power, the Kingdom of Tonga has also never lost its indigenous governance and remains a constitutional monarchy. Known as "The Friendly Isles," the people are strongly Christian, and are hospitable and helpful.

Tonga is geologically old and has a barrier reef that blocks the ocean's waves, resulting in calm waters within the island groups. An almost constant, gentle breeze keeps the otherwise high temperatures pleasant.

After a good night's rest, we took the dinghy ashore the next morning and explored Neiafu. It's small, but is actually the second-largest town in Tonga. We were impressed with the cleanliness, so different from Pago Pago. The Tongans seemed calm and friendly and were constantly sweeping the wooden sidewalks and packed-earthen streets. Pigs wandered around at will. I wasn't sure where they did their business, but we didn't see any pig-doo along the streets. We saw pigs, all different colors and sizes, on church steps, sidewalks, streets, in yards, never fenced in. They were apparently a part of the community.

Pigs had their useful purpose. People didn't mow lawns; pigs kept them neat and trim. They ate much of the soft garbage, like fallen fruit. And, of course, pigs provided meat.

Neiafu looked like how we imagined an American frontier town would have looked 150 years ago. Little shops stood side by side with wide open doorways leading to dark interiors with high ceilings. Stocked shelves stood behind the counters. Customers told the clerk at the counter what they wanted and the clerk took items off the shelf. Merchants spoke little English. Prices weren't too bad, but we were glad we had such a good supply of staples.

We stopped to have a hamburger at a little restaurant run by an American. No doubt, the majority of his business was yachties. There were about 20 boats anchored in the harbor, but only about half of them had people living aboard. We ate at a tiny outdoor table and watched the townspeople go about their day.

Saturday would be market day, so we planned to stay anchored off Neiafu until then. Soon we would be joined in Tonga by Jack and Donna, Vern and Connie and others we'd met along the way.

Being able to move around on solid ground or non-rocking boat helped my tender rib. We were relieved to be there, allowing time for me to heal.

While out and about the tiny town, we ran into a family we'd briefly met in Samoa. Hal, Kim and their teenage son, Don, were on a whirlwind trip aboard their beautiful 48-foot sailboat, *Kim Thu*. Hal was a doctor from the Seattle area. Kim was a Vietnamese he met in Vietnam, where he had been a flight surgeon and she a nurse. They had a house near Seattle and would return there after this trip. Their boat was one of the nicest I'd seen, with conveniences not usually found on sailboats.

We heard there would be a parade through town on Saturday and several of us yachties gathered to watch it. It consisted of two small pickup trucks, one carrying Boy Scouts and the other an award-winning weaver. The weaver excited me because it was the very one that Fanny, my weaving instructor in Samoa, had talked about. Her truck was a sight, with woven items swinging from every conceivable place: mats, bowls, trays, and baskets of all sizes.

The weaver's truck didn't stop, but I inquired and found her little shop a couple of days later. We talked about our mutual friend in Samoa and I showed her a little of my work. She appeared to be impressed, much to my gratification, although to her it probably looked like the work of a nine-year-old. She said she'd never before known a yachtie to take weaving seriously. She gave me some dyed dark brown and black pandanus leaves and I bought several leaves of white from her. In Samoa the only color I ever saw was the natural light tan. I would never achieve the skill level of this weaver. For one thing, her weaving was so tiny, her vases could hold water. Her designs were intricate and perfectly symmetrical. When I wove in a different color, it was all I could manage to keep a stripe evenly spaced. This woman had been weaving all her life and came from a long line of weavers. It was fascinating to see her work and talk with her.

We left Vava'u to explore the outer islands. Neiafu on Vava'u would be a sort of headquarters for us, where we would shop or sometimes meet other boaters, but we wanted to spend most of our time enjoying the solitude and beauty that surrounded us.

Once we anchored off an island with a long protected point with only two houses on it. From our boat we could see a woman walking to a well and home again. I rowed ashore in the dinghy to meet this older woman whose name was Marie. Rather than talking, our exchange was really more of a mime since she knew very little English and I knew no Tongan. Much of the week she lived a simple, quiet life alone on the island, but on weekends others came to gather coconuts and to dig clams. I gave Marie gifts of a packet of sewing needles and a card of pretty buttons, and from her broad smile I could tell she was pleased. These items were not readily available in Tonga.

Marie signaled for me to wait and she stepped into her square hut made of palm fronds. The woman emerged with a string of reddish-black beads. Showing me the tree from which the berries came, she picked up a fallen one from the ground and a rock. Rubbing the berry against the rock, she showed me how she polished the dried berry to make the beads. The necklace was threaded on a strong, thin vine.

The old woman asked if I liked oranges and we walked to a small orange grove. Oranges indigenous to that area are green when they are ripe, have tough skins and many seeds. Reaching for a knife from a holder around her waist, she whittled away the skin and handed me the orange to eat while she fixed one for herself. She wanted me to call on her niece, a public health nurse, who lived in Neiafu. I promised her I would.

I stood to leave and Marie walked me back to my dinghy. I had in the boat an empty green, four-liter wine bottle. In this strongly Christian community, I wasn't sure that an empty wine bottle would be an appropriate gift, but I hated to throw it away and had left it in the dinghy. When I asked her if she would like to have it, her eyes lit up. "Oh, yes. Wonderful!" For the next several days, from the boat we saw Marie walk back and forth to the well with her green bottle.

The next morning I rowed the dinghy to Neiafu and found the public health nurse's home. Marie's niece answered the door, expecting me. I was surprised when I saw two shiny needles pinned to her collar. Ruth spoke English and told me her aunt had shared my gift with her. She also mentioned how pleased she was that I had called on her aunt and thanked me for my kindness in taking the time. I knew Ruth had children and I'd brought gifts of an inflatable world globe and a few packages of dried fruit. The children squealed with delight when they saw the globe. The nurse, too, was excited. Her husband was a teacher and he'd be able to show it to his students.

The next evening, we heard a loud knocking on our hull. The nurse's husband, Nuku, stopped by in his skiff to invite Bruce to go fishing with him the next day. We invited him aboard. Nuku had never been aboard a large sailboat and was curious about everything—how we cooked, navigated, the engine, the sails. He was a handsome man, tall and strong with sparkling eyes and good humor. Nuku taught school on a neighboring island and fished on his way home from work. The next day he swung by to pick up Bruce and they trolled in his skiff for about an hour and caught four fish, two barracuda and two tuna. The teacher tried to give all four to Bruce, but Bruce declined saying we had no refrigeration, but that we would enjoy one of the tuna.

As it turned out, my little trip to see Marie developed into three friendships and enriched our stay in Tonga. I was so glad I'd made the effort.

We soaked up the peaceful, quiet atmosphere in Tonga, such a contrast from Samoa. The only sounds we heard were waves lapping against the boat and an occasional bird's screech. Even in town, it was quiet and peaceful. Once we lingered by a church and listened to the choir rehearse. They sang a cappella in strong, rich harmony.

Tongans were handsome people and friendly toward us. The women wore long wrap-around skirts and a sleeveless or short sleeve top, then usually another cloth around their waist that covered their hips. The men wore long wrap-arounds too, and usually something around their mid-section that was made of tapa cloth.

A Tongan in a large canoe stopped by to invite us to a feast. For a small fee we enjoyed several kinds of fish and a pig stuffed with fruit, then wrapped in pandanus leaves and baked in an umu, a large pit. We were the only people there from a private yacht, the others were from chartered yachts.

As they arrived on their boats from Samoa, we were reunited with our friends Vern and Connie, Jack and Donna, and within a few more days three more boats came in, people we knew from Samoa. We celebrated our reunion by motoring in our dinghies to a German restaurant that the doctor who had looked at my rib had told us about. We also invited the doctor and his wife. The restaurant, though a bit expensive, was a real treat. The owner was a German, married to a Tongan woman. They lived upstairs in the same building, with their two daughters.

Jack and Donna anchored near *Impunity* and the next day we snorkeled with them in the clear water. I added several nice shells to my collection, hanging them off the back of the boat in a mesh bag until they were cleaned out. While snorkeling, we never tired of watching fish darting around the multi-colored coral. I finally got my prized cowrie that I'd been hoping for, a three-plus-inch tiger, so my shell collection was complete. Tonga is a treasure-trove for shell collectors.

Every few days we moved the boat to a new island and anchorage, sometimes near other people, sometimes alone. We kept in touch with the others on VHF radio. Without doubt, Tonga was the prize landfall, with the south, quiet side of Tahiti a close second. Our days passed pleasantly with lots of snorkeling, reading, weaving, and simply being in a heavenly location.

Off one of the uninhabited islands where we regularly anchored, we often rowed ashore to feed a couple of piglets. Because of their coloration, we called one of the piglets Stars and the other Stripes. The mother stayed clear of us, hovering in nearby bushes, ready to protect her babies. We enjoyed the little pigs and saved our kitchen scraps for them.

One late afternoon while we were anchored on the eastern edge of the Vava'u group, a strong wind picked up, pushing the boat toward the lee shore. Bruce put out a second anchor, placing the two anchors about 60-degrees apart. Even with two anchors, we worried that the boat could run aground in this exposed anchorage. We stood anchor watch all night, using our normal watch system of four hours on, four hours off, to make sure *Impunity* was safe.

Bruce berated himself for not moving the boat earlier to a more protected anchorage. We were alone, but were sure that Jack and Donna would have known better and were in a safer situation. The next morning after the weather calmed down, Bruce talked to Jack on VHF radio. Much to our amusement, Jack said they'd been up all night, too, making sure *Zingara's* anchors held. He admitted saying to Donna, "I know Bruce wouldn't have put their boat in jeopardy like this!"

Once or twice a week we motored our dinghy over to Neiafu to pick up and send mail, then if Saturday, go to the market. We marveled at the fresh produce: tomatoes, green peppers, carrots, bananas, papaya, pineapple, mango, avocado, watermelon, cantaloupe, onions, potatoes and eggs. The fresh produce, plus our freshly-caught fish and the staples we had on hand, kept us eating like royalty.

One day, with Jack and Donna, we took our dinghies to a tiny uninhabited island that looked like a postcard. We were certain that it had been used as a movie set, it was so perfect. Bruce had caught a nice tuna and we built a fire on the beach and grilled the tuna over coals. Donna had made a salad and we had fresh bakery bread. Jack cracked open a bottle of wine and we feasted to our hearts' content.

Our original plan was to stay in the Kingdom of Tonga for four weeks, but it was such a paradise, we decided to make it six weeks and forego some of the smaller islands we'd originally planned to visit. We definitely wanted to be in Hawaii by late June, giving us a month for the final leg of the journey. We still had 6,000 nautical miles of ocean to sail.

Bruce readied the boat for the long slog home, checking the engine, the electronics, the propane fuel lines, and etcetera. He examined each sail and, by hand, re-stitched a few spots. Two of the jibs had badly worn bronze hanks, which he replaced from our stock of spare parts. One of our galley water pumps had been requiring many more strokes to deliver water, so he disassembled it and replaced seals, using extras we had brought.

In the meantime I rearranged our food supplies, getting our stores handy for when we sailed in rough seas. Our supplies were in good shape and all we had to provision was fresh produce and bread.

Jack and Donna came over for breakfast, then, armed with scrapers, we four cleaned *Impunity*'s hull of the many critters clinging to it. We wore our snorkel gear so we could get to the bottom of the hull. This would help us make faster time. We were anchored over a sandy bottom in about 30 feet of water. As we scraped, the barnacles and worm tubes slowly sank. It was a surreal sight, hovering weightless in the warm, extremely clear water, watching the small whitish bits slowly drift down. We offered to help clean Jack and Donna's hull, but they'd met and made friends with a local professional diver and preferred to hire him to do it.

Finally, it was time to say farewell to Tonga and our friends there. Jack would be a couple of days behind us. Although they sailed from their home in Hawaii to the South Pacific together, Donna was prone to severe seasickness, so much so that at sea she could rarely leave her bunk. They decided that Donna would fly home and Jack would single-hand back. It wasn't ideal, but for them the most practical.

Vern and Connie aboard *Tainui* would be sailing on to Indonesia where he had been Peace Corps staff.

Bruce paid special attention to the high seas weather forecasts from Arnold each day. Though the region was still transitioning out of hurricane season, conditions sounded reasonably good for the next several days.

A final farewell dinner at the German restaurant, and we were off the next morning. We cleared customs and were on our way. Almost right away Bruce put out the fishing line and we caught a six-pound tuna. Nice!

The four days from Tonga to Samoa were dicey either with flaky winds, no winds, or strong squalls.

187

We alternated sailing and motoring, finally reaching Pago Pago on Saturday morning. We refueled, took on water and some fresh produce, bread and pilot crackers, and departed American Samoa for Hawaii on Tuesday, May 22, 1990.

This leg of the journey would likely be the hardest sailing and we would be beating, going against the wind. Neither of us looked forward to it.

Feeding "Stars & Stripes"

Tongan using charcoal to paint tapa cloth

12

Man Overboard!

Log Entry—June 20, 1990: Man Overboard!

We remained firm believers in the watch system. Four hours on, four hours off worked for us and we maintained that schedule throughout our trip. With only two people on board, it was an ideal arrangement.

If we did things right, *Impunity* took care of herself, making the night watch quite pleasant. Waves rose and fell, larger swells rose and fell, rocking the boat accordingly. It seemed that every hour and a half

Bruce with tonight's dinner

a wave almost twice the normal size would present itself, definitely getting our attention, and then the seas would return to a regular pattern. *Impunity's* heading wandered to port and starboard a bit, but stayed true to course, leaving our tasks to watch for

191

problems, weather, or traffic. The weather was overcast with intermittent rain.

Around 3:00 a.m. Bruce called me from the deck. He needed my help. Our steering vane had become partially detached from the boat. If Bruce couldn't repair it, or worse, if we lost it altogether, it would mean having to hand-steer for the rest of the journey. Hand-steering makes a watch a real chore because you can't leave the wheel or tiller without going off course.

Working upside down in the dark, his face inches from the rolling sea, Bruce hung over the transom to replace bolts while I shined the flashlight for him and held onto the seat of his pants to keep him from falling in. After about 20 minutes of fitting and tightening bolts, all the while upside down, he made the repair and reset the wind vane, and we were off again. Losing the vane wouldn't have been life-threatening, but it would have been extremely inconvenient.

Again, we were thankful for our strict watch system. If no one had been on deck keeping watch and making routine checks on the equipment, the problem would likely have gone unnoticed until it was too late to save the vane. This was yet another affirmation of having spare parts on board for all the important systems on the boat, and a reminder of the importance of a sailor knowing his boat intimately.

Although our lengthy stay in Tonga had ruled out stopping at some islands, we planned to visit the tiny island of Palmyra, the only incorporated territory of the United States. In World War II, it was used as a military base, but today it's generally uninhabited except for scientific projects or brief visits by cruisers. Another couple we knew from Samoa was currently there and we were in radio contact with them. The weather was terrible they said, and suggested we not bother going out of our way to get there. During good weather Palmyra was a tropical delight, but it wasn't much fun during stormy weather. We decided to sail on.

Bruce often put out the fish line and almost always caught a fish. One morning he pulled in a big yellowfin tuna, about five feet long and weighing about 100 pounds. We were afraid to bring it aboard for fear its thrashing around could injure one of us.

While Bruce hung on to the struggling fish, he called, "Mary, bring me my gun." When at sea, we kept our weapons handy in the event of pirates. I quickly brought his handgun and he shot the big fish. For a couple of days we had tuna for breakfast (creamed on pan-fried toast), lunch (mixed with mayonnaise, served open face on pilot crackers) and dinner (tuna steaks with rice). We didn't put out the fish line for a few days after that.

For a couple of days, the weather took a nice turn for the better and I enjoyed my favorite perch in the stern. My 10:00 to 2:00 night watch was blissful and I was thankful not to be bashed around. At 1:00, during my routine check, I spotted lights from a large ship on the horizon. Although we were the privileged vessel, because of our position relative to the ship and because we were under sail, I kept my eye on the ship. I took bearings repeatedly and after a period of time could see that we were on a collision course.

I hated to wake Bruce, but it was our rule. In situations like this, he never grumbled about being awakened. We monitored the approaching ship together, and it appeared as though they didn't see us, even though we'd shown our deck lights. The ship made no attempt to change course.

Bruce called on the VHF radio. "To eastbound ship on my port bow, this is the sailing vessel *Impunity*. Over." Nothing.

A few minutes later Bruce called again. "To east-bound ship on my port bow, this is the sailing vessel *Impunity*. Please state your intentions. Over." No answer.

A third call and still no response.

Because we were the privileged vessel, we were obligated to maintain course and speed. But finally, when we could see that the ship was not going to change course, we had to alter our course in order to avoid a collision. We tacked and went around and behind the ship.

After the collision danger was past and we were back on course, *Impunity* received a call on the VHF. The caller spoke in a heavily accented voice. He identified his ship as a Japanese freighter heading for the Panama Canal. The captain, possibly the only English-speaking person on board, was apparently asleep when we first called on the radio. Afterward, Bruce, relieved, joked to me, "I thought they were going to make sushi out of us." In truth, they could easily have hit us, and it is entirely possible that they would not even have known it. They apparently were keeping neither a visual, nor radar, nor radio watch. To them we might have been merely a bump in the night.

The weather turned rough again. As we beat windward against the 25- to 30-knot trade winds, the boat's bone-jarring action became almost intolerable, with the bow climbing up and then crashing down with every wave. Bruce struggled to achieve easting to keep us on the course to Hawaii, adjusting sails and our course to make the most progress east while sailing north. Each day seemed to get rougher. We donned our foul weather gear, not because of cold, but to protect our skin that had grown sensitive from continuous salt spray.

194

Cooking was tough. As a routine procedure, I strapped myself into the galley, but still had to hang on to the counter with one hand while trying to prepare a meal. During one bad-weather patch, I handed up our plates of beef hash with a side of green beans to Bruce in the cockpit. I sat down beside him on the starboard bench, a cushion-covered cockpit locker, and started to eat when a wave came over the side and drenched my plate. I didn't have the strength or desire to cook something else. I simply poured the salt-water off my plate and ate what I could. Bruce's food was untouched by spray and he shared his with me. Neither one of us even spoke about it—it was too grim for words. We were tired of fighting the weather, fighting for easting, even having to fight just to eat dinner.

A tropical storm passed south of us, making our lives more difficult. By this time we were seasoned sailors, but this crappy weather made it tough going. Everything we did took supreme effort. Of the many legs of our journey, this 3,000-mile Pago Pago to Hawaii run was turning out to be the worst. More than once I thought that if this had been the first leg of the journey it would have been our last.

On June 6 we crossed the Equator and said hello to the North Pacific. It was a sure sign that we were on our way home.

I noticed a strange feeling when I knelt on my right knee. I saw that my leg from shin to knee was swollen. I didn't recall a particular blow, but we were getting bashed around on a regular basis. I must have bumped my leg. It didn't really hurt, but my leg had a tight, swollen feeling and felt spongy to the touch.

On the 29th day, at the end of my morning 6:00 to 10:00 watch, I was anxious to get Bruce up on deck. *Impunity* hummed with built-up pressure. Over the last several hours, the wind had steadily built to 30-plus knots. Seas were getting larger, the lee rail was nearly always under water. Every few seconds we punched through yet another swell and crashed into the trough behind it. We were pushing the boat too hard, causing stress on the gear.

At sea, we again alternated sleeping in the midship bunk. I gently touched Bruce's shoulder. His eyes flew open as he immediately awoke. I doubted if he ever slept soundly while at sea. He'd only slept an hour, but that would have to last until he could sleep during my late afternoon watch.

"We need to shorten sail, we're going too fast," I said.

He climbed out of the bunk, holding the overhead railing to steady himself. "Okay, I'll be right up."

On deck, Bruce slipped on his life vest and harness, glanced at the compass to confirm our course, watched the rough seas for a moment, noting steaks of foam atop 10- to 12-foot waves, and surveyed the already shortened mainsail. He stepped to the upper deck, and eased the halyard. Leaning against the boom to free both hands, he pulled the mainsail down, preparing to take in another reef.

I remained in the cockpit to handle the halyard. I heard a loud bang, a noise I'd never heard on the boat.

I looked up. "Bruce, what was that?" He wasn't there. "Bruce!" The upper deck was empty.

I let out a garbled scream. My worst nightmare! The thought of being alone on the boat terrified me. I could never manage the boat without Bruce. I didn't *want* to manage without Bruce.

I forced myself to think. I had mentally rehearsed the man overboard scenario often enough. I always knew our reciprocal course—180 degrees from the direction we were headed—so I'd know how to reverse our direction. I had to start the engine. I had to drop the sails or they would work against me. I had to throw out the man-overboard pole, but I had to see him first, so he could get to it. Wait a minute! Was there an electronic signal on the pole that I was supposed to set? *Oh, God, I can't remember!* My mind screamed with panic, even as I thought through the steps to be taken. I visually swept the seas behind *Impunity.*

If one of us had to fall overboard, I'd hoped it would be me. I knew Bruce could find me. I wasn't so sure I had the skills to find him.

And now, where was he? I scanned the rough seas. I'd lost him already! Something yellow caught my eye. I ran to the railing and there he was, under water but struggling to reach the surface. His lifeline still held him, but it was wrapped around his leg and dragging him feet first at six to seven knots. As a large wave brought him to within reaching distance of me, I frantically grabbed the shoulder strap of his harness and strained to keep his head out of the water. The first thing he saw was my terrified face. He gasped for air, but I saw relief in his eyes.

The lifeline that was wrapped around his leg made it difficult to maneuver. I pulled him by the shoulder strap past the cockpit winches where the railing wasn't so high. Luckily, we were heeled to port so the distance between us wasn't as great as it would have been had he fallen off the starboard side.

Bruce freed his leg while I desperately hung on to his harness. In dead calm, *Impunity's* deck was three feet from the water, but this sea wasn't calm. Bruce took advantage of a rising swell and grabbed the toe rail, allowing me to reach the front of his harness. Leaning against the winch, I pulled his harness with both hands with all my strength while he hoisted himself up. Together, we pulled him aboard, exhausted. Neither of us could have done it alone.

It was the happiest day of my life. As *Impunity* sailed under jib alone, we clung to one another for several minutes, laughing, kissing and marveling how lucky we were. I thanked God for His help.

The boom rested on the railing. The topping lift, a line from the masthead to the outboard end of the boom, had broken while Bruce began tying the third row of reef points. The noise I'd heard was the boom hitting the railing. When the boom dropped, it flipped Bruce into the sea.

To continue sailing, Bruce lifted the boom and settled it on a notch on top of the dodger, but because of the weather we weren't using the mainsail anyway. We were doing six knots with the jib alone.

Nothing seemed so bad after that close brush with disaster. We endured the rough seas, happy in the knowledge we had each other and that we were less than 300 miles from Hawaii. When we could both be on deck, we talked about our future, or read aloud from our James Herriott books.

We kept our daily Maritime Mobile Net schedule via ham radio, reporting our position and weather conditions. After the net, we occasionally made contact with the family through helpful land-based ham operators. We didn't indicate to the family how tough the conditions were, or about Bruce falling overboard. Each day Bruce listened to at least two high seas weather reports.

Our twice-daily contact with Jack told us he was wearing down. His voice slurred from exhaustion. He wasn't getting nearly enough sleep, only minutes at a time. We worried about him. This leg of the journey was tough for two of us. We couldn't imagine doing it alone.

We encountered more ship traffic as we neared Hawaii. The weather was warm, at times downright hot. We shed our foul-weather gear

We began to see cumulus with some patches of stratus clouds, indications of islands close by. Sea birds flew overhead, another indication of land.

The wind dropped as we passed through the wind shadow of the "big Island" of Hawaii, and we motored for several hours. At midnight, June 23, we sighted the island of Oahu! We stood off for the rest of the night so that we could approach Ali Wai Yacht Harbor in daylight.

We were in America! After clearing customs and immigration, we stepped ashore, letting our legs adjust to a solid surface. We had been in radio contact with Donna, and she met us at the Ali Wai Harbor. She was obviously worried about Jack. She, too, knew how exhausted he was and was anxious to get him home.

A nurse, Donna looked at my leg and said I really needed to see a doctor. She suggested one that was within walking distance of the harbor and, using a pay phone, I made an appointment for the next morning.

We promised Donna we'd be there for Jack when he came in, probably two days hence.

We used the harbor's shower, cut each other's hair, and the next morning I saw the doctor. My leg hadn't gotten worse, but it was still swollen and discolored.

The doctor looked at my leg from the doorway as he entered the examination room, raised his eyebrows and said, "This is how people lose legs. If that leg isn't better within 24 hours, you'll be admitted into the hospital."

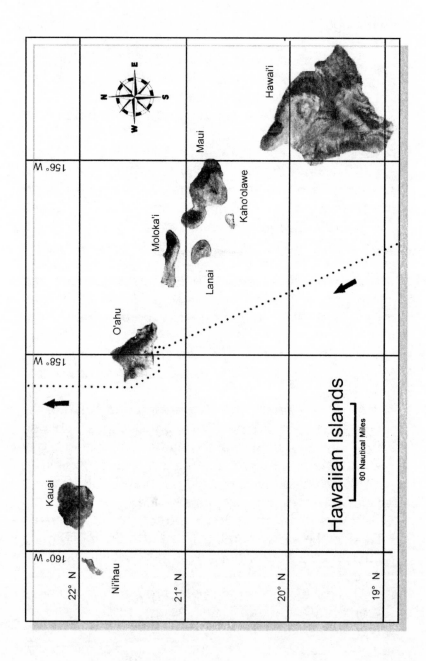

Hawaiian Islands

60 Nautical Miles

Hawai'i

Maui

Kaho'olawe

Moloka'i

Lanai

O'ahu

Kauai

Ni'ihau

156° W

158° W

160° W

22° N

21° N

20° N

19° N

Yikes! "But it doesn't even hurt!"

The doctor shook his head. It was mysterious because there was no broken skin. He examined it and asked about a possible injury while at sea.

"It's hard to say. We were both getting bashed around out there, but I don't remember any specific time when I injured my leg."

"Something is causing this swelling and we can't ignore it." He prescribed a strong antibiotic, ordered me to elevate the leg for several hours each day, and to apply cold packs. He told me to come back the next day. I followed his orders, but the next day it wasn't noticeably improved. He agreed to give it another day. Thankfully, by the next day the swelling was down enough that he felt I was past danger. It continued to improve. We never did find out what had caused the swelling.

Jack radioed that he was outside the harbor, and Bruce replied we were there to take his lines. The poor guy was almost incoherent with exhaustion. He steered *Zingara* unsteadily to the slip, tossed his lines to Bruce, who secured the lines, then climbed aboard *Zingara* to shut off the engine and electronics.

Jack and Donna had a poignant reunion and she took him home. They invited us to visit them, after giving Jack a few days to recover.

Having known Jack and Donna so well while in Samoa and Tonga, I loved seeing their home in Hawaii. It was large and airy and we luxuriated in having space and enjoying Donna's wonderful cooking.

Jack recovered from his ordeal quickly. He was a strong, well built man, who took good care of himself. He was a retired school superintendent, having come up from the ranks as a teacher.

We discussed the 32-day Samoa to Hawaii ordeal. Jack looked very serious. "I've sailed single-handed around the world, but these last 32 days were the hardest thing I've ever done." He shook his head. "It was really tough."

I looked at him in disbelief. "Tough? *Jack*, it was a fucking nightmare!"

The "f" word isn't really a part of my vocabulary. Jack and Donna both looked startled. So did Bruce.

Jack nodded. "It was. It was a fucking nightmare."

Mary picking from a stalk of bananas

13

A Dream Fulfilled

Log Entry—August 5, 1990: Land Ho! We can just make out the mountains of Vancouver Island.

*O*ur two weeks in Hawaii passed quickly. This wasn't a touristy visit, but rather a time for recuperation and preparation. I had previously lived in Hawaii for two years, and Bruce and I had taken the girls to Hawaii more recently. This time in Hawaii was merely a stopover to get things done for the next leg of the journey. We readied the boat, got together with Jack and Donna, and managed a couple of shopping excursions for boat supplies.

After studying our pilot charts for the northeastern Pacific, it was clear that July and August were the foggiest months. Celestial navigation requires a clear, definite horizon so we knew we could not rely on celestial alone when approaching the rugged northwest U.S. coastline. Bruce felt we needed a Loran-C to navigate through the fog for those times when celestial navigation would not be possible. We discounted GPS as a practical option since those in current use were far from reliable and much more expensive than Loran-C.

Bruce repaired the topping lift, going aloft in the bosun's chair. I again arranged our supplies so that they'd be handy at sea. We topped up our propane, water and fuel, and put in a supply of fresh fruits, vegetables, and bread.

We departed Ali Wai Yacht Harbor at noon, July 8, 1990 with Jack handling our lines. Turning west out of Ali Wai Harbor, we made good time in brisk trade winds. Soon we swung to the north in the Kauai Channel, keeping a few miles off Oahu's west coast. Kaena Point slid behind us as we settled back into our four on, four off watch routine. Only 2,280 nautical miles to Cape Flattery, Washington. Chicken soup simmered in the pressure cooker. Donna had sent raspberry scones for the next morning's breakfast.

Feeling rested, I was more relaxed leaving for this leg than I'd ever felt when going to sea. Maybe it was that we were heading home. Sailing conditions were perfect, the high seas forecast good, and we were assured we'd make good time. The weather was ideal and we wore shorts and tee-shirts.

A day out of Honolulu and we were again alone with nothing but the sea stretching out in all directions. Night watches were a delight. The only sounds were seas parting as *Impunity* sliced through waves, and the occasional roar of distant waves breaking from their own weight. The sails, full of wind and trimmed to maximum efficiency, propelled us forward as if *Impunity* wanted to get home, fast.

On about the fifth day, we spotted a commercial fishing boat. We turned on the VHF radio in time to hear, "Gettin' crowded out here." It was a lone fisherman, probably eager for a little human talk. He asked if we were fishing and Bruce mentioned that we had caught a nice 20-pound mahi-mahi, sometimes called dolphinfish. "That's more than I'm catchin'," he said in a slow drawl.

As we pushed north, the weather cooled and we began wearing warmer clothes with foul-weather gear and knit hats for night watches. We brought the sleeping bags up from below deck storage. Even a wool blanket wasn't enough. We continued to alternate sleeping in the midship bunk.

Bruce was pleased with the Loran-C, but used his celestial navigation to compare results. When turned on, the Loran-C continually gave us our position. Loran-C calculates positions by measuring the time difference between low frequency radio signals broadcast from Loran-C stations on shore. When signals were strong, it was quite accurate, and by using both Loran-C and celestial navigation, when possible, and comparing the results, we had confidence that our position and course were correct. This would be important as we approached the sometimes unforgiving entrance to Washington's Strait of Juan de Fuca

Flying fish occasionally found their way to our deck. We threw them back into the water right away, if we saw or heard them land. One morning we found a 6-inch squid, complete with ink, on the deck. It was hard to imagine how that happened. Waves seldom broke over the deck.

We had a few light squalls and partially gray skies, but the sailing was smooth and blissfully uneventful.

For a few days the winds were very light and we motored to make forward progress and to keep the boat from wallowing. It was a relief when wind again filled the sails, pulling us energetically toward home.

We began making plans for when we returned. Bruce intended to return to the marine electronic field. We definitely wanted to live in a rural area. After reading so much James Herriot, we couldn't wait to get a dog. I wasn't wild about the idea of a long commute, though taking Safeco up on its offer to again work there as a programmer/analyst had its attractions.

"Mary," Bruce said, "why don't you consider writing? People enjoy your letters. You could write for sailing magazines." The more I thought about that, the more attractive it became. We began brain-storming topics.

But first we had to reverse our original plan. We'd sold the house to buy a boat, now we needed to sell the boat to buy a house. We considered keeping *Impunity* and still buying a house, but we wanted to be in a position to make a large down payment on a home. Besides, *Impunity* was overkill for Puget Sound; she was a sea-going vessel. Over the years we had seen so many boats tied up at marinas, never used, year after year. Boats are expensive to moor and maintain. We'd done what we set out to do. It was time to move on.

There were a lot of unknowns ahead in our lives, but after 13,000 miles at sea, we were used to that.

A large ship passed us, an unusual occurrence. Bruce spoke with the captain via VHF and learned they were on their way from Los Angeles to Japan. Bruce asked for their position and compared it to our Loran-C fix and they coincided.

Our heading was straight north with the intention of avoiding the North Pacific High, a semi-permanent, subtropical high pressure area located in the north-eastern portion of the Pacific Ocean, west of California. Our plan was to skirt around, leaving it to starboard, then, once passed, turn east. To go through the North Pacific High meant there would be no wind.

I spotted a glass Japanese fishing float bobbing in the water. Bruce maneuvered the boat around so that I could bring it aboard. It was covered with barnacles, but was in good shape. Then we found what appeared to be brand new float, a lovely shiny green, about 12 inches wide. Within the next few days we found another glass float and a few plastic ones. We collected the glass ones, but ignored the plastic. It appeared the glass balls were caught in the North Pacific High and they were effectively "circling the drain."

Glass balls weren't the only thing floating in the North Pacific. We saw large cans, bottles, and what appeared to be ship's garbage. The litter in these pristine waters made us sad.

When the wind died or was squirrelly, we motored. One night we shut down the engine, double-reefed the main and drifted. Both the air and sea temperature were 69 degrees, cold compared to the South Pacific.

July 20 we experienced total calm and overcast, but after a couple of days, we welcomed light 3 knot winds. We crossed the 42nd parallel, the same latitude as the California-Oregon border, though several hundred miles away.

On July 24, we passed the midway point with less than 1,300 nautical miles to go.

We both marveled at the ease of this leg of the journey. The winds were weak allowing us both to relax and enjoy this last leg of the journey. Bruce was generally pleased with the Loran-C, though it wasn't always accurate, depending on where it picked up its signals: Hawaii, Alaska or the North Pacific chain.

We finally put to good use the radar detector that Bruce's folks had given us. On much of our South Pacific journey we didn't use it. Ships there often didn't use their radar, which is unsettling. As it happens, they lease their radar by the hour so when they are in the open sea, it isn't even on. But now that we were approaching an area where we were likely to encounter other ship traffic, we kept our radar detector on. The alarm sounded as a freighter appeared on the horizon heading from Los Angeles to Taiwan. Bruce asked for their position, explaining we were using a new Loran-C.

As we crossed shipping lanes, ship traffic picked up and by listening to radio conversations and occasionally getting alarms from our radar detector, we learned that we were one of four boats in the area, but we rarely saw any of them.

As we neared the Washington coast, the winds were directly astern of us, making the "boat look like those knock-down clowns that kids like," Bruce noted in the log. Interestingly, my attitude about that had relaxed, and so had my stomach.

On August 3 we spotted several magnificent gray whales headed west, their warm breath condensing in the cold air.

I was impressed with Bruce's calculations regarding our fuel supply. He had two spare 5-gallon containers of diesel and had added 22 gallons of fuel in Honolulu. Since then we had run the engine 68 hours. We still had plenty of fuel to last, even if we needed to run the engine in the Strait of Juan de Fuca.

We began experiencing northwest fog. We appreciated the Loran-C, especially since it was now getting strong signals from the U.S. west coast.

We cheered when we spotted land, 26 days after we set sail from Hawaii. We could barely make out the mountains of Vancouver Island on our port bow. Within a few hours, through the fog we sighted Tatoosh Island. There it was! The northwest tip of the continental United States!

After 13,000 miles at sea, we were almost home. My mind raced and I was filled with mixed emotions. I felt elation, but also a sort of a let-down. Our adventure was coming to an end. What we had so carefully planned and worked for, and then actually accomplished, was almost finished.

This had been an extraordinary journey, one that few people make. We'd sacrificed to make it happen, but we persevered. After 14 months, we were different people than when we left home. We'd experienced joy and had seen sights and been to places most people only see in pictures. But we'd also experienced fear, discouragement and discomfort. I'd found strength I didn't know I had. I'd learned that I could be miserably uncomfortable, lacking sleep, and still function. I could put out a decent meal in rough seas when I had to hang on with one hand for dear life and could barely keep from throwing up. I had an even deeper respect for Bruce and his all-around seamanship and ability to solve problems.

We knew unequivocally that we could rely on each other. Using our watch system we knew the person on watch, no matter what time of day or night, would do what was necessary to keep us safe. If we took care of the boat, she would take care of us. We could sail with impunity.

Our lives were richer because of this experience. Our marriage had more depth and meaning. At sea, we had only each other and we found that to be enough.

As we neared our home state, the fog became so thick visibility was almost zero. It was spooky not being able to see anything, yet moving forward. We frequently checked the Loran-C for our position, plotted it on the chart and made small course adjustments to stay out of the shipping lanes, and to stay clear of land. We heard ship traffic on the radio and could hear ships' engines rumbling. Bruce occasionally called on the radio to make sure they saw us on their radars.

"Yes, we see you on radar, *Impunity*. You're off our starboard bow."

Proceeding up the Strait, we cleared Point Wilson on August 7 and were officially back in Puget Sound. We docked at Port Townsend. The kids were planning a welcome home party for us the next day and we planned to greet them by sailing into Shilshole Marina.

In Port Townsend we tidied up the boat, I cut Bruce's hair, but then went to a salon for a shampoo and hair cut. We luxuriated in the marina's showers.

The next morning we were underway and arrived at Shilshole exactly on time, twelve noon. We heard the family laughing in delight as they spotted us coming in under sail. They waved and ran down the guest dock in a swarm. Although I laughed, too, I had tears in my eyes and a lump in my throat. What a grand reunion with Bruce's folks and all the kids and grandkids. The family had again reserved a section of a Shilshole restaurant for a luncheon celebrating our return.

We'd done it! We'd fulfilled another dream. Not without struggle and doubt. Not without sacrifice, but we'd done it. We felt tremendous relief and satisfaction, and yes, pride.

We looked forward to a new beginning.

Epilogue

*A*fter returning home from cruising the South Pacific, Bruce again worked in the marine electronics field as a product manager, enriched with his own experiences at sea.

I followed Bruce's suggestion and began writing articles about long-distance cruising, keeping a good watch system, the value of household bleach on board, planning meals for an extended voyage, and other topics of interest to sailors. After a few rejections, three different magazines published my work in the same month. That success gave me the self-confidence to consider writing as a profession.

Camping has always been one of our favorite things to do, but we like to move from place to place, rarely spending two nights at one camp. It became tiring breaking down and setting up a tent with every move. We acquired a camper, the type that fits on a truck's bed. It has been perfect for us. Sailing articles morphed into RV articles and my writing career was firmly launched.

While camping we look for article material. Bruce's camera is always at the ready, while I take notes as we go along. A two-week camping trip usually produces three to five articles. Those articles, plus articles about other events we attend, and issues of interest to homeowners, produce several pieces published each year in magazines and newspapers.

Because we have a goal other than just having fun while camping, we look at places and situations with closer attention, knowing that what we're seeing and experiencing may end up in print. We delve into the history, the flora and fauna, and things to do in the surrounding area. This research results in a far richer experience for us.

One summer in eastern Oregon on our annual two-week camping trip, I spotted a girl, probably in her teens, walking along a rural highway with a huge pack on her back. She looked weary and hot. My mind whirled with reasons she might be out in the country, by herself, back-packing. I would never know her story, but I made up one of my own. My first novel, *Rosemount*, was born that day. I finished *Rosemount* and found a publisher. However, Leslie, the character in *Rosemount*, wouldn't leave me alone. Her story wasn't finished, I discovered, so I wrote a sequel, *McClellan's Bluff*.

While researching cattle ranching in Washington for *Rosemount*, I visited a rancher in eastern Washington. He made several references to the Mount St. Helens' eruption of 1980 and the disruption that event caused his cattle operation. *Tenderfoot*, a romantic suspense with a sub-plot of the Mount St. Helens eruption, was my third novel.

Although it had been on my mind, I had never written of Bruce's and my experiences in Africa with the Peace Corps. Although I had reservations about the self-exposure that memoirs create. I tip-toed carefully into our story and, refreshing my memory with letters written to family at home, realized the story would interest people who liked to travel and to learn about other cultures. The gamble paid off. *Tubob: Two Years in West Africa with the Peace Corps* has brought me many opportunities to speak to groups about life in a third-world country. By this time, Bruce and I felt we knew the publishing business pretty well, so we decided to self-publish the memoir and have been happy with the results.

That brings us up to our experiences aboard *Impunity*. This book was a joy to write. As I wrote, feelings of exultation welled up, but then so would memories of desperation and despair. I relived these moments as I prepared to share them with you. Again, we decided to self-publish this book, making our own decisions on the different aspects of publishing.

Being a writer has enriched my life. I've made contacts and life-long friends with other writers, people whom I deeply respect. It's gratifying to have someone come up to me in a grocery store and tell me they enjoyed a book or article that I wrote. Someone has noticed, and that's important to me.

I'm honored when invited to speak at library and community groups. I'm sure every writer is thrilled when asked to attend a book club when the selection being discussed is her own. Speaking to groups about *Tubob: Two Years in West Africa with the Peace Corps* has opened many opportunities to discuss conditions in Africa and how basic the needs there are. My presentations also lead to discussions about Peace Corps opportunities for "older" recruits, people with experience who could make a difference.

As planned, we sold *Impunity* and are living on rural acreage on Camano Island, Washington, in Puget Sound. And of course, we have the dog we longed for, a chocolate Lab, Toby.

Glossary of Nautical Terminology

Aboard: On or in a boat

Aft: Toward the stern. Sometimes referred to as "After."

Anchor: A device usually of metal attached to a ship or boat by a chain and cast overboard to hold it in a particular place either by its weight or by its flukes.

Awning: A tarp that's designed to provide shade.

Backstay: Standing rigging that runs from the mast to either the boat's transom or rear quarter, counteracting the forestay and jib.

Beam: The width, or diameter, of the boat.

Beam reach: Sailing at a 90-degree angle to the wind.

Beat or Beating: Sailing as close as possible to the direction from which the wind is coming.

Below: As in "going below decks" meaning going to the space below the main deck.

Berth: A bed on a boat.

Bilge: The lowest inner part of a boat's hull.

Binnacle: The stand on which the boat's compass is mounted.

Block: A single or multiple pulley.

Block and Tackle: A system of two or more pulleys with a rope or cable threaded between them, usually used to lift or pull heavy loads or sails.

Boarding Ladder: A ladder hung from the boat's side to facilitate getting on and off a boat.

Boat: A small craft compared to a ship, which is usually considered a commercial vessel.

Boom: Spar (pole), along the foot (bottom edge) of a fore and aft rigged sail.

Boot stripe: Stripe painted just above the waterline to evaluate the boat's trim.

Bosun's Chair: A seat, usually made of canvas, used to hoist a person up the mast.

Bow: The forward end of a vessel (normally, the pointy end).

Bow Pulpit: An extension of the forward deck encircled by a stainless steel handrail.

Bowsprit: A spar extending forward from a ship's bow, to which the forestays are fastened.

Brightwork: The exposed metal or varnished woodwork on a boat.

Broach: To slide sideways down a steep wave, rendering the boat out of control.

Broad reach: Sailing with the wind coming from behind the beam.

Bulkhead: Walls or partitions.

Bulwark: The railing extending along the sides of the boat above the deck.

Cabin sole: The floor of the cabin.

Celestial navigation: Navigating by the sun and stars using a sextant which measures the angles between the stars or sun and the horizon.

Channel 16: An emergency and hailing channel on the VHF radio.

Cleat: An object of wood or metal having one or two projecting horns. Used for tying off a boat's line.

Clew: The free corner of a sail not attached to any standard rigging.

Close reach: Sailing farther off the wind than beating, facilitated by letting out more sail.

Cockpit: A recessed area in the main deck where the boat is steered, usually in the middle or rear of the boat, normally large enough for seating for the crew.

Companionway: The entrance to the cabin. The passageway that leads from the cockpit down into the cabin.

Cutter: A single-masted boat, rigged fore and aft.

Deck: What you walk on aboard a boat or ship.

Depth sounder: Electronic echo-location device to measure water depth.

Dinghy: A small boat made of either hard or inflatable material used to transport crew or passengers from their anchored boat to land.

Dodger: A canvas or wooden cover (sometimes a wooden frame covered with canvas), usually covering the width of the cockpit and extended aft.

Drogue: Any of several heavy devices lowered into the water to slow a vessel.

EPIRB: Emergency Position Indicating Radio Beacon. A device that sends out a radio signal to alert search and rescue services.

Foredeck: Part of the deck that lies forward of the mast.

Forecastle: Pronounced "fo'c's'l," Under the foredeck of a vessel, often where the boat's sleeping quarters are situated.

Foremast: A mast forward of the mainmast of a sailing vessel.

Forestay: A steel cable that runs from the top of the mast to the tip of the bowsprit to support the mast.

Freeboard: The part of the hull that is above water.

Galley: The boat's kitchen.

Gimbal: Hinges on which stove, compass or lamp hangs that help to keep them level as the boat rolls.

GPS: Global Positioning System A satellite-based navigation system that uses transmitted signals and mathematical triangulation to pinpoint location.

Ground tackle: An anchor for boats.

Halyard: A line run through a pulley up the mast that is used to hoist a sail or flag.

Hatch: An opening into the boat, as a doorway would be to a house.

Hawsepipe: A deck opening near the bow of the boat where the anchor chain passes through.

Head: A marine toilet or bathroom.

Heave to: A maneuver to stop or slow down a boat in rough weather by setting the sails to keep the bow pointed toward the wind.

Heeling: Boat leaning to one side due to wind pressure.

Helm: The steering mechanism, either a wheel or tiller

Hull: The watertight body of a ship or boat.

Jib: A triangular staysail that sets ahead of the foremast.

Jibe: To change course by bringing the stern across the wind.

Keel: A structure, usually weighted with lead, that extends vertically into the water below the boat to provide stability.

Knot meter: A instrument mounted in the cockpit that shows the speed of the boat in relation to the water, and distance traveled.

Ladder: A boat's staircase.

Lazerette: A large storage area in the stern of the boat.

Lee cloth: A piece of material such as canvas or netting from the side or bottom of a berth to the overhead to keep a sleeper in the berth.

Leeward: Downwind from the point of reference. Opposite of windward.

Lifeline: A line usually about 6 feet long attached to a harness worn by a sailor. The lifeline can be clipped to padeyes that are bolted to key areas of the boat. Lifeline is also a term for the wire railing on a boat.

List: Leaning to one side due to an uneven load.

Line: A length of rope. There is no "rope" on a boat, only "line."

Log: A running written record of the boat's activities, including position, speed, taking on fuel, making repairs.

Loran-C: A radio navigation system that allows a receiver to determine its position by listening to low frequency radio signals transmitted by fixed land-based radio beacons.

Mainsail: Sail located behind the main mast of a sailing vessel.

Mainsheet: The line that adjusts the mainsail.

Mast: A tall spar erected more or less vertically on the center-line of a boat.

Overhead: The boat's ceiling.

Padeye: A device bolted or welded to the deck that a line, such as a safety or lifeline, runs through.

Poop Deck: The aft-most, raised weather deck on a ship.

Pooped: When a wave or seas break over the stern of the boat.

Port: The left side of the boat when facing forward.

Porthole: A boat window that can be opened

Portlight: A boat window that cannot be opened.

RDF: Radio Direction Finder, a navigational aid establishing a fix by means of the bearings of two known radio station signals.

Reef or Reefing: Reducing the size of the sail to make it smaller in strong winds.

Rode: Rope or chain attached to the anchor.

Roller furling: A method of rolling up or letting out the jib from the cockpit, rather than manually from the foredeck.

Rudder: A flat, movable piece of wood or metal attached to a boat, used for steering.

Run: Sailing downwind with the wind coming from directly behind the boat.

Sat Nav: Satellite navigation system that gives the boat's position.

Schooner: A sailing boat with two or more masts, typically the foremast smaller than the main mast.

Scupper: An opening in the side of a boat at deck level to allow water to run off.

Self-steering gear: Equipment used on ships and boats to maintain a chosen course without constant human action.

Sheet: A line (rope) that is used to control the movable corners (clews) of a sail.

Sloop: A sailing vessel with a single mast and a fore- and aft-rig.

SSB: Single Sideband Radio. A radio that can transmit and receive over thousands of miles, such as a ham radio.

Stanchion: Stainless steel short vertical poles that run along the perimeter of a boat's deck through which lifelines run.

Snubber: A stretchable line attached between two long pieces of rode to absorb anchor line strain and soften the impact of waves or tidal pull.

Spar: A pole made of wood, metal or lightweight materials used to support sails.

Starboard: The right side of the boat when facing forward.

Staysail: An auxiliary sail, often triangular, set on a forestay.

Stern: The rear of a vessel.

Tack: To change course by bringing the bow across the wind when sailing windward.

Transom: The back of the boat, the most aft part of the boat.

V-berth: A V-shaped bunk in the bow.

VHF radio: A short-distance radio with a range of about 20 miles used for ship to ship communication.

Waterline: The line where the hull meets the surface of the water.

Windvane: A flat paddle that catches the wind's direction and automatically adjusts the self-steering gear.

Windward: Upwind from the point of reference. Opposite of leeward.

Wing and wing: A way to set the sails so that they extend straight out from the sides of the boat, using the boom and whisker pole.

Whisker pole: An aluminum pole that hooks onto the mast to hold the jib to take advantage of wind coming from behind for downwind sailing.

Yawl: A two-masted fore- and aft-rigged sailboat with the mizzen mast located aft of the rudder post.

Acknowledgments

So many people have contributed to my writing vocation, it would be impossible to list them all. Certainly, my husband Bruce is at the top of the list. His encouragement has given me the freedom to follow my heart's desire. Monetary concerns are low on Bruce's list of priorities, which is a good thing, as most writers will tell you. In addition to his moral support, Bruce, as my first reader, has helped me develop ideas into a readable form. Bruce also has taken on the task of graphic design for my last three books. Sailing with *Impunity's* graphics have been extensive and time-consuming.

My deepest thanks and appreciation to Patricia Bloom and Robert Mottram for their time and expertise in helping me fine-tune this memoir. They have gone far beyond friendship to help me make *Sailing with Impunity* all it could be.

My critique group–Mary Ann Hayes, Gloria MacKay, Erika Madden, Margo Peterson, Lani Schonberg, Val Schroeder, Peggy Wendel and Darlene Dubay--have been a constant source of inspiration and encouragement, sprinkled with gentle constructive criticism. I don't send out anything, books, articles, even blog posts, without first running them past my critique group.

My children, Byron, Jeffrey, Bonnie and Robin, and my extended family, have given me strength through their love and devotion. I am so thankful for them. My friends and my writing community have cheered me on, giving me their nod of approval and guidance, allowing me to proceed with confidence.

My deepest thanks to you all.

About the Author

Award-winning author Mary E. Trimble, in addition to sailing the South Pacific, served for two years in Africa with the Peace Corps, and more recently retired from the American Red Cross after volunteering for 20 years. Her experiences also include crewing on the tall ship *M.S. Explorer* as purser and ship's diver, and she served as Admission Director for a professional deep-sea diving school. After obtaining a degree in Computer Science, she worked as a programmer/analyst at the corporate headquarters of a large insurance company. *Sailing with Impunity* is Trimble's fifth book and second memoir. More than 400 of her articles have appeared in numerous publications. She and her husband, Bruce, enjoy rural life on Camano Island, Washington.

www.MaryTrimbleBooks.com